Why You Are Not Selling As Much As You Should…

Or Could…

Or Perhaps, As Much As You Deserve to.

ISBN 978-0-578-03679-3

Printed in the United States of America.

September 2009

Contents

I am not a sales god. I don't, for a moment, think that I have all of the answers.

That said, I have had *some* success as a salesman, as a sales manager, and as a sales trainer.

Very early in my sales career, I discovered that I got my particular buzz from feeling as though I had helped a customer. This meant more to me than my relative position among the other salesmen. When I became a sales manager, I quickly developed a fondness for helping other salesmen to succeed, even in small ways. Just as with customers, I saw that some needs were individual, and some were global. In those times when I was able to work with a particular salesman to uncover his own weakness, and then develop a program to strengthen it, I felt as though I had truly accomplished something.

Over the years, I have discovered two things:

1. There really is no "University of Sales." The sales people that are looking to be educated in their field search the bookstores for new ideas and better habits. They ask questions about improvement all of the time. They attend seminars that they hope will help them. This was certainly true of me, and lots of other sales people that I met.

2. Sales people, as a rule, talk too much, or say too much about the wrong stuff. They waste a lot of customer's time, and a great deal more of their own, thinking that the key to selling is based only on having a cool way to say something. The art and science of finding a problem to fix before you try to fix it, is unknown, or poorly implemented, much of the time. I see this as the biggest obstacle that salesmen create for themselves.

In my efforts to help salesmen, based on those two challenges, I have written more than two hundred thousand words, over a twenty-five-year span. I have written on these topics, along with every other obstacle I could think of in the world of selling.

The reading public will never see most of these words. Too much of what I wrote became preachy, or too cerebral. When I would share chunks of my work with sales people whose opinion I respect, they always seemed to gain the most from the most simple and basic suggestions.

I have also received a fair amount of encouragement over the years to "write a book about selling." I found this to be particularly true of sales people that found some worth in the three-day seminars that I sometimes lead.

So, I would try, and fail, and try again.

The tiny little epiphany that encouraged me to start again, the kernel of thought that became the genesis for this book, was this statement from a salesman.

"You can help me sell more. You always did when I worked for you. You helped me see that my weaknesses could always be improved, and when I did, I had created a new weakness to improve."

I had the great opportunity to work for many years for a good guy, who is incredibly smart. He can also be a tough son of a bitch, and I mean that as a compliment. He has created a great deal of wealth for himself, and more for others, with his great disdain for the status quo. He seems to have the necessity to figure out what is wrong with something, and then improve on it.

I began to discover how this could benefit me personally, when I received my very first annual review, working for the company that he owned.
In most of the reviews that I had received in the past, someone told me, quite subjectively, either what I did well, or what I did poorly. I think that these kinds of reviews are based usually, in the mind of the boss, that people are too sensitive to be criticized, or they are lazy and stupid, and need a stick on the head once a year. Neither style ever motivated me to do better.

This review was different. My boss gave me the review form and told me to study it. He told me to fill it out, and be prepared to go over it in two weeks.

Before I read it, I was of course prepared to give myself high marks in everything, so that I could argue for a big raise. I was quite surprised as I studied the form.

My job was divided up into nine areas. The most important task was to decide which three areas were my best, which were the worst, and which three were in the middle.

I recall being wowed by both the objectivity of this approach, and the difficulty of the task. The hard part was making the decisions about what belonged in each category. Making the comments was a breeze.

In two weeks, I sat with my boss, each with our review forms completed. I was astonished, although I don't know why, that they were nearly identical. The only disagreement was that one category that I had as best, he called middle, and vice versa.

We had instant agreement over where my weaknesses were. It was quite easy for us to get to work on specific plans to improve my weakest areas. He made a few comments for improvement about my middle areas. The "best" topics became rather unimportant.

We decided on some milestones, to keep me on task throughout the year.

This objective way of looking at things made a great impact on me, in the way that it was so forthright, and so objective. No time at all was spent in comparing me to anyone but myself.

I recall him saying, "Even if your worst areas are better than another persons best, they are still the areas that are holding you back."

The last words of the interview process were these. "I expect you to have completely different worse areas next year."

That is the approach that I have tried to take in this book. I have attempted to outline the areas that can have the biggest negative potential for you, and offer a few pointers to improve on them. If you find yourself reading about a problem that you don't have, feel free to skip over it. My hope is that you will be able to identify your own area of greatest weakness, your own biggest obstacles, and find some ways to strengthen your skills.

If you read this entire book, and find nothing of merit, nothing of use, and nothing worth remembering, I apologize for wasting your time. If you cannot make just one more sale from something that I have discussed in this book, send it back to me and I will refund your money.

If you do find anything of worth, please tell all of your friends in sales.

In creating this book, I have used stories, true tales, as a way of illustrating a point. I have told these stories to the best of my memory, but the names have been changed.

If you recognize a story about yourself, it could be you, or it could be only a coincidence.

One final comment, as an apology. Throughout this book, I use the terms salesman and salesmen. Perhaps I should have written salesperson, but I didn't. It is not a sexist remark; the book is intended for those who work at the noble task of selling, of all sexes.

Chapter 1.

Are You Meant To Be in Sales?

Not everyone is cut out for a life in sales. To test this, think of some really smart, successful people that you know, and you can easily identify that some of them would be lousy sales people.

In my years as sales manager, I certainly hired some people that weren't cut out for sales, although they thought they were. Nearly every one of these people was attracted to the world of selling because they thought it was easy, and that pretty much all you had to do was to show up, and people would buy stuff.

How can you tell if you belong in sales? Here are some qualities that I seem to find as universal among the great sales people that I have known.

1. Independence. A job in sales is about as close as you can get to being in your own business, without having to make the investment that a business owner must make. Think about that. If you own your own business, you are highly independent, and are on 100% commission. If you are willing to trade a salary for independence, and the freedom to make as much as you can earn, it might be the job for you.

2. A strong work ethic. The people that are attracted to sales because they are lazy never seem to make much money. If you are willing to maximize the few and precious hours of the day when you can be engaged with customers, and spend early mornings, and time after five P.M., organizing, studying, doing paperwork, and all of the other things that you need to do away from customers, this might be the job for you.

3. Organized. If you don't mind being your own file clerk and secretary, if you insist on efficiency in time and materials, this might be the right job for you.

4. Fun. One of the things that I looked for when interviewing a salesperson was an element of fun. Not the great jokester type, but the attractive quality that fun people have. It was fairly easy to measure; I just asked myself if I enjoyed being

with this person for half an hour. If you don't enjoy the company of others, than they won't enjoy being with you. Get a job with a cubicle, you'll be happier.

I once had a conversation with a sales recruiter. I was asking him about a new policy that my employer had established that made it a requirement that all of the new sales hires needed to have a degree in engineering.
I was a bit concerned about this, as many engineers that I have known were, well, dull.
I told him about my concerns, saying that it seemed that many engineers might also become accountants, and I just didn't see many of these people fitting into a sales career.

The recruiter clearly understood my concern, and agreed that the majority of engineers would lack whatever the unknown ingredient is that successful sales people seem to have. He said to me, "Think about it this way. Imagine you went into a large engineering department. Place yourself in a position to see and hear all of the engineers at the same time. Assume that they are good engineers, and good employees. Just observe until the one 'wild man' makes himself known to you. He will be the person that all of the other engineers find themselves attracted to, although they don't know why. That's the one."

That's as good an explanation as any.

There does seem to be a certain quality that someone has, that makes the rest of us enjoy his or her company. I'm not saying that a salesman is supposed to be a jokester, or the life of the party all the time. That is certainly not true. Perhaps it is the self-confidence that great salesmen display that draws us to them. Maybe it is the way that we admire successful people that seem to show humility along with their confidence.
I know that I can't define it properly, but I know it when I see it.

The one thing that I can say with surety about the truly successful salesman that I have known is this. They are all, by the definitions of Dr. Maslow, highly actualized people.

Carl had been employed for about six months with us, and this was his first job in sales. He was a sharp guy, with a clear interest in learning. Of all the people that I have hired, he was the one that asked for the most support, and he always seemed to be putting it to good use. Carl asked for, and received, regular field workdays with me, which often tired me out by the amount that he "picked my brain."

He was a good employee, and I was optimistic enough about his future to send him to the corporate offices for a week long training session.

While the trainees were at the home office for this training, my boss would spend some time with each trainee, getting to know them. He would also receive briefings from the trainer, regarding the progress of each trainee.

I was quite surprised when he told me that he just didn't see Carl as having much of a chance of making it.

Of course, I immediately began to defend him.

My boss explained the source of his concerns, as soon as I shut up. The trainer had observed that during the training, Carl quoted me endlessly. When a point was made in training, he would comment on whether I seemed to agree or disagree with the point that was being made. He would make comments about how well I used the suggestions that were raised in the training.

The boss went on to say what he had observed, when they went out to dinner together, that not only did he quote me, but that he had taken on my mannerisms!

I had not noticed these things, but I conceded to the wisdom of my boss.

"This is what you want to look for," he said. "If he is going to make it, he will have to accent and empower his own strengths. That's a lot different from imitating someone."

Within a few months, I could see that my boss was correct. The clearest indicator was in Carl's inability to think on his feet. If he was in a situation that was new, and was tough for him, he was lost. Perhaps I was flattered by the way that he came to me so often for advice. Perhaps I was impressed by the way that he always wanted to know what I thought, so that he could do better next time.

The truth was, he didn't have enough self-confidence to believe that he could make himself into a successful salesman.

Self-actualized folks don't imitate others. However, that doesn't mean that they don't emulate them. In fact, I believe that highly successful people are big-time emulators. Don't they always seem to be asking questions about how someone accomplished something? Aren't they always studying ways to get better? I can certainly tell you that when I observe someone doing something that they are far better at then me, I copy them, and without a bit of shame.

When Chuck was a salesman on the street, he was the very best. He was far too humble to ever tell a customer this, but for many years, he was the top salesman in a company with a field sales force of more than 300.
I was surprised to learn, after Chuck had moved on to start his own business, that he was once told that he should give up sales. The salesman that told me this story was a big fan of Chuck's, and went on to become the top salesman himself.
He once asked Chuck what his secret was, particularly since he had heard the legendary story of the national sales manager encouraging Chuck to find a different career.
Chuck's answer was rather simple.
He said that he had always been pretty shy, and he knew that even when he said the right words, they didn't come out in a very powerful or convincing way. Therefore, he took public speaking classes to help him with his confidence. The other thing that he did was this. He paid attention to the best qualities of the most successful salesman around him, and then he just did what they did. Of course, he did them in his own way.

Are you proud of what you do?
An interesting phenomenon, that I have witnessed many times, is that some people actually seemed to be ashamed to be a salesman! Perhaps that explains why there are business cards for salesmen that say things like "account representative," and "customer product interface specialist."

Let's face the fact. We are salesmen, no matter what they call us. I know that there are probably more slugs per capita in our field than in most others, but that is just something we have to accept. We need to accept also that we probably do just what our customers do. When we finally find an insurance salesman, or a car salesman, that does a good job, we see him as a good guy, and we willingly refer him to our friends.

It's quite easy to figure out what we dislike in sales people ourselves, and easier yet to avoid doing the things that they do to irritate us.

I firmly believe that if you are proud of your employer, and proud of your products, it shows through. As does the opposite. I also know that I have earned very nice rewards in my selling career, far more than if I had stayed with my plan to be a mechanical engineer. One thing that I am distinctly proud of is this. Regardless of the considerable sums that I was paid for my efforts, my customers *always* made more money on their investment, than I received in commission for it. Helping others to create wealth is something of which you can be proud. It affects not just them, but their families, and larger groups of employees.

Speaking of being proud of being in sales, here is another person to consider.

At the request of a fellow manager, I did a second interview with a potential hire for a job in sales.
I gave him very high marks, and fully expected that he would be hired. When we talked on the phone a few weeks later, I was surprised at what the manager told me. He said he had gone to meet the spouse, and that the spouse was clearly not eager to say that she would be proud of saying that her significant other was a sales person.
He reasoned that at some point, the salesperson would have to please the family, and leave sales.
Perhaps he was right, I am unsure. However, I know that any job decision is a family decision, and should be considered as such. If your home situation is one where our noble profession is looked at dimly, you should not ignore it. If your family is not comfortable with the ups and downs in income that all salespeople live with, it just might not be the field for you.

A final comment on this topic.

A wise man once told me that he believes this one statement as much as he believes anything.

" In any debate or discussion between rational people, the best idea always wins. "

I have come to believe this heartily. In addition, there is another belief that I associate with it, and that has to do with will, passion, and persuasion.

Consider the fact that when Columbus was circling the globe, the Flat Earth Society was still signing up new members.

The Flat Earth people were just wrong; they weren't stupid.
In the end, they all changed their minds.
In all of those cases where you can see that your customers are clearly "doing it wrong," they are doing so, based on their current beliefs. How do those beliefs get changed?

How *does* the best idea win?

In every selling situation, somebody convinces someone else of something. In most cases, the customers convince us that they have no need for our products or services.

What is different in those other cases? In basic terms, the salesperson believes that he is right, more than the customer does. That's what happens when we are persuaded to change our mind. There seems to be a transfer of enthusiasm from salesman to prospect.

On every sales force, there is a superstar. Some salespeople will whine endlessly about some imagined advantaged that Mr. Supersalesman has.
Others want to know what his "secret" is.
As this story will hopefully explain, it's not a secret.

J.P. was a year or so into his career, and had learned to admire the success of the one guy who always seemed to have his name at the top of the stacks.
As it happened, his family had a vacation home in Mr. Superstars territory, and J.P. asked me if I thought it would be possible to ride around with him for a day while he was on vacation, to see what he could learn.

I admired him for wanting to see what the secret was, and encouraged him to contact the salesman and ask him directly. Being the team guy that he is, permission was immediately granted; although there was a caveat that J.P. had to make sure that he didn't interfere with the workday.
This was the story that J.P. told, about what he learned.
"First off, I was surprised at how rural the territory was, even though he was fairly familiar with the area.
I noticed that there was far more distance between customers than in my own territory.
I noticed that the day started early, and ended late, and lunchtime was used for traveling to the next customer."

To his surprise, Mr. Superstar was an affable guy that was fairly humble about his success, giving a lot of credit to the great products that he had to offer.

The **big** discovery was this. J.P. heard all of the same objections and excuses that he heard from his own customers, every day. What was clearly different was that they weren't seen as some huge obstacle that had to be overcome. They were listened to, and then dealt with clearly.

Mr. Superstar never wavered in his belief about the products, and his will and his passionate belief for his products persuaded customers to, at the very least, think about them in a different and more positive way.

One particularly argumentative customer simply didn't seem to be willing to budge an inch on his beliefs.

With a smile, he was told, "You know, you're just not getting what I am saying, so let me start over."

He then told a story about a very similar situation, and the success that this other guy was having by using his product solutions.

I guess that it has to do with what you believe in, and how much you believe it, huh?

Chapter 2

Are You Organized?

There are two ways in which you have to be organized. One is your approach to selling, and the other is your stuff. They go completely hand-in-hand, so they need to be dealt with together.

The *primary* focus of this chapter is about organizing your stuff.

Your *stuff* is defined as the method that you use to organize the movement of a customer through a sales process, along with your plan about what to do next, and when.

This is important for two reasons:

1. You don't need notes that say "Stopped to see a guy, he bought everything I have, no further need to visit." Rather, you need to comment on the process, immediately after each sales call, when it is fresh in your mind. If you do so, you will actually begin to depend on your own notes.
2. If you don't, you might forget. In fact, I guarantee that you won't remember everything. It is impossible to remember all of the details of a full day of sales calls, and record them at the end of the day. If you want proof, spend one day, recording the following things at the end of each sales call:
   - Whom you met with, that is, everyone on the call.
   - What you discussed, particularly what problems they are encountering.
   - What products you introduced.
   - Any other details of the call that are important, other topics that were discussed.
   - Where they are in the sales process.
   - What you agreed to do next.
   - When you should follow up.

Then try doing the same thing at the end of the day, or worse yet, the next day. You will be surprised at how sketchy the details are, and how the calls can run together in your memory.

If you try this and get the results that I fully expect that you will, you would be a fool to continue in any other way than what you now know is the only way to accurately record the important work that you have done.

John was a pretty good salesman, at least when he was in front of the customer. I did notice that he refused to make any notes after a call, and I also noticed that when he made return visits, he had no plan. He was the type that thought he would figure it out when he got there. After one particularly good sales call, I was astonished that he never made a single note about what I saw to be a fairly complicated process that would involve many calls, many products, and several locations. He had agreed to do certain and specific things for several people.

"John," I said. "Aren't you going to write anything down about all of the work that has to be done here?"
He thought for a moment and said, "Do you think that I am going to forget?"

"Well, if you do," I asked, "How would you know?"

Assuming that you are in a sales situation that involves more than one product, and multiple calls, organized record keeping replaces your memory, and keeps you, and your customer, on plan.

I am a strong believer that the professional salesman closes every call with a plan of action that is agreed on *during the current call*. This can be very specific, or it can be as vague as to continue trying to discover an application for your product.

It's quite easy to do this when the customer is enthusiastic about learning more, or doing more. If so, your notes would say something like "Call on the 15th to confirm demo appointment for the 20th."

However, it's not always so clear, nor is the customer enthusiastic, yet. Maybe you have covered all of the ground that you could for today, or maybe you have just run out of time.
The question to keep in your mind is, "What is the next step?"
The truth often seems to be that the customer is intrigued, but not dedicated to buying. That makes it a process, right?

So you say something like, "I think I am beginning to see some application for our products here, but I really need to understand more, in order to provide a clear suggestion. Why don't I come back in a month, and we'll discuss it some more?"

The customer will do one of three things:

1. Agree.
2. Disagree, and have a better idea, or more suitable time frame. He might also reveal some need or application that you were unaware of.
3. Tell you that there is no further reason for discussion.

Any of these things are good; because you now understand how your customer views the time, and the work that you have shared.

After that, **be sure to write it down, and then take responsibility for executing the plan.**

A wise boss once told me that if you want to differentiate yourself from all of the knuckleheaded salesmen out there, it's as easy as this:

Find something to do for a customer, promise him you will, and then do it. Whenever possible, exceed their expectations.

That takes us to the note taking and organization stuff. You need the following tools:

1. A place to record it.
2. A method for you to be reminded.

Supposing, in the example above, the customer agreed with your suggestion to move forward.

The organized salesman has some system that provides an alarm about work to be done, and what the work is, along with the appropriate notes about what was important, and to whom.

If so, he is then armed with the ability to call the customer in three weeks to say:

"Hello Bill, according to my notes from our last meeting, we agreed to get together in a month to discuss our products and your application. That puts us at next week. How is Tuesday afternoon for you?"

Whatever the customer says at this point will be helpful to you both, even if he says, "What was your product again?"
You both will clearly know where the project is, as well as your customer's understanding about you, and your products.

Jack was a knowledgeable salesman that depended on his highly technical abilities to get results. He believed that he so impressed customers with this, that they would simply call on him when they wanted to know more.
I was with him when he stopped in to see a customer a few months after his initial visit, which he was convinced had huge potential.

"Hi Tom," he said, handing over a business card. "I wanted to stop back and see what was happening on that big project. You seemed really interested in our big expensive widget."
The customer handed Jack back the card with these words. "First off, the name is Bill. Secondly, I told you that we would be deciding within a few months. We did, a few weeks ago."

Jack didn't have a single note to refer to. He was astonished that the customer had not called him.

There are many ways to keep good notes. For some guys, it is nothing more than a book that they write all of their notes in, and read through over and over. This wouldn't be my choice, but some salesmen make it work.

You can use any of the selling software that is out there, and there are some excellent ones. Of course, none of these are worth a damn if you don't record things properly.

Many sales books, managers, and teachers talk about the "Sales Funnel."
Simply put, this means that there is a process to go through, and that there are many more customers in the beginning of the sales process than at the end of it.
If this is true, (and it is) your own daily planning should reflect this. This is what I mean:

Every day, you should be working to bring the sales process to the ultimate goal. An order. Clearly, however, you won't be writing business on every call.

As you plan each workday, try to create a mix of calls that move everyone that you see a little closer to the sale, but from all of the different parts of the funnel. Take the time to visit a brand-new prospect every day. See some customers that are a little farther along in the process.

Wade sold a reasonable number of products every year, but he was not happy with his overall results, or the money he was making. He invited me for a ride-around day to observe his actions. I told him that I would wait until the workday was over before offering any advice or suggestions.

It was a strenuous day. It did result in one order, but I certainly noticed that Wade was pushing too hard on some customers that simply weren't ready to buy, for a variety of reasons. His actions and his presentations were professional and powerful.

At the end of the day, when Wade was eager for my observations, I asked him if this was a typical workday. He thought that it was. I asked him when he saw prospects that were new to him, and when he made calls that were more introductory to his products and services.

He said that he only did this when he didn't have anyone left to close. He was enthusiastic about saying that "he was a closer," and that he didn't have time for cold calls.

I asked Wade how much potential was in his territory. He was thoughtful, and offered an answer that I knew to be ridiculously low. I told him that he needed to do a little homework, before I could really offer any advice.

I asked him to research how many potential customers he had in his territory, and how many he had been actively engaged with, in each of the last three months. It took him about a week to answer.

Wade was astonished that there were probably triple the prospects in his territory than he had guessed there were. He also discovered

that in each month, he was seeing a very, very low number of
customers, some of them over and over, without results.
I have never been an advocate of the "Nifty Fifty" approach that is
intended to hammer away at customers until they relent, or hide.
Therefore, I was pleased with what Wade discovered.
" It happens every time," he said. "I get a few orders, and then I see
that no one else is very close to buying, so I turn up the juice on a
few guys that just might be close."

"I would be way better off planning to see customers in each stage
of the selling process, every day."
And he was.

Something that I learned in my own selling days that I have passed
along to any salesman that would listen is this:

You will know that you are properly closing every call, if when you
get back to your car, or when you hang up the phone, you can write
down what to do next, and when. If you can't, you have not given
the customer the impression that there has been any progress. Just as
importantly, you have not demonstrated any reason to continue.
I often found it very helpful to record *exactly* what the customer said
when we got to that stage. I would record the comments in quotation
marks so I knew who said it. It makes for a powerful tool that I call:

"The Reason I'm Here"

I developed the habit of saying "The reason I'm here," at the
beginning of every sales call in the process. It seemed to lend
importance to the phone call or visit. Here are a few examples of the
benefit of "The Reason I'm Here," and of quoting the customer.

1. The reason I'm calling today is this. Last month, when I
   suggested a product demonstration, you said, "Let me talk to
   a few people and see who is interested in knowing more."
2. The reason I'm here today is that the last time I visited, you
   said to "See you in a few months, some changes might be
   occurring."
3. The reason I am sending this e-mail, is that you said, "Shoot
   me an e-mail next week, and I'll let you know how the
   approval is going."

Summary

1. Make notes after every call. Record whom you spoke to and about what. Make notes about the customer's particular interests, motivations, and hot buttons.
2. The only notes that will have any value will be the ones that you can make while the call is fresh in your mind. If you don't think this is true, trying making all of your notes at the end of the sales day. You will be astonished at what you can't remember.
3. If you closed the call properly, you will be able to clearly record what you are going to do next, and when.
4. Create a system that will provide alarms to remind you about upcoming work.
5. Review your notes; you will learn to trust them.
6. The next time that you call or visit the customer, you will be able to remind the customer all about where you are in the process, and why he should speak with you now.

Chapter 3

Are You Worth Listening to?

It has surprised me, on more than one occasion, how unprepared salesmen can be when they get a chance to do what they like to do best, which is talk.

Scott was a better than average salesman. One of the brightest and most articulate guys I have known. He was someone that I admired in the way that he could present ideas.

On a ride around day, Scott decided to stop into the XYZ Huge Company. He explained that it was the kind of place where you had to meet with engineering to get anything accomplished, but that first you had to become acquainted with the folks in purchasing. He went on to say that this often required lots of visits, and lobby sitting. He explained how you would wait twenty minutes, and then the purchasing agent would call you on the lobby phone, with instructions to drop off literature, and stop back next month. While we waited in the lobby, we chatted idly about baseball, or something completely unrelated to work.
After about fifteen minutes, a man approached us, holding the business card that Scott had given to the receptionist.
"Are you Scott?" He asked.
Scott stammered out something brilliant like, "Um, yes."
"What can I do for you?" Mr. Purchasing Agent asked.
Due to his unpreparedness, Scott stumbled, stammered, and stuttered unintelligibly for a few moments. It was embarrassing for everyone, Scott in particular. The Purchasing Agent took pity on the man, and finally Scott was able to get out a few words about the reason for his visit.
When the response was that he would pass some literature along to Engineering to see if they were interested, Scott happily handed some over, without even bothering to learn whom the engineering contacts might be.
We walked back to the car in silence. Once safely inside, Scott began banging his head against the steering wheel repeatedly. I didn't feel that a lecture on being prepared was necessary.

I once read that the only tools that a salesman really has, are his words. They should be maintained, and kept sharp and oiled.

It has become my firm belief that a salesman should never introduce a particular product, or group of products, until he knows what problem they will solve for the customer.

Of course, this excludes those presentations that you make that provide an overview of your products or services, but beyond that, products should wait to be introduced until they are put in the framework of solving the problem that you learned about, using your superior interviewing skills.

However, once you do get a chance to speak, to hold forth, to shower the customer with your endless product knowledge, shouldn't you be prepared?

On the other hand, are you one of those guys that prefers to "wing it?"

I was taught that people will only follow only one thing, and that is a *compelling vision*. The people that have changed the world have offered that to us, and folks have lined up behind them in support. A compelling vision illustrates how your life will become better if you are willing to make a change.

Too often, when a salesperson gets the opportunity to present his products and ideas, he offers no more than a pretty good idea. People just don't follow a pretty good idea.

When the time finally comes for you to hold forth; Be Prepared!

If you were giving a sermon, a speech, an obituary, or asking someone to marry you, you would certainly take time crafting and word smithing your presentation, to be as powerful, convincing, and compelling as possible, right?

Are your sales presentations less important?
Martin Luther King said, "I have a dream." I can't imagine him getting people to march with him if he had said, "I have a pretty good idea," or "I have a suggestion."

You no doubt have certain presentations that you have made countless times. I'm sure that you have crafted these powerful statements, just by repetition, and by observing what the customer responds to enthusiastically.

There are always a few questions that come up over and over in every salesman's life. You know, the ones that you can almost begin answering before the customer can complete the question.

These are usually a common misunderstanding or drawback of your product. I'm sure that your answer is complete, concise, and persuasive. Compelling. Compelling, because repetition has caused you to practice your response.

The point is that the best salesmen have practiced and polished EVERY presentation. They have thought about the customer's point of view on those tricky questions, and fashioned a great response.

The best sales people write them down, and they practice them over and over, reshaping the words and sentences until they are satisfied.

By the way, this long and hard work is always done thoughtfully while driving, while in airports and airplanes, and before or after those few and precious selling hours.

When you have finally earned the opportunity to speak, you get to teach someone, and not before.

Make the most of it.

Create those compelling presentations, and continue to reshape them every day. And every day, your presentations will get a little better. As I have said, repeatedly, it is best to hold back on the talking until the customer is intrigued to hear what you have to say. You will know it is that time if:

1. You understand what the customer is trying to accomplish, and how you can help.
2. You have requested, and received permission, to present your ideas.

Keep in mind that it's not only about products. There are often many choices that a customer has to alleviate his problems. It is his job to calculate and decide which choice is best for him, and which is the best value. Because there are different types of solutions, there are different ideas, and that is important to discuss with them.

If your product does something this way, and another one does it that way, it is because they are based on different *ideas.*

Ideas are at the root of the solution, and taking time to discuss your ideas should be enlightening to customers, particularly in highly competitive situations. Don't let the customer decide that your way is inferior, only because it is different from the one he knows.

Take time in your presentation to discuss the roots of the product, or the way it is marketed, and how the customer will benefit from that idea.

Why do you sell in those quantities, and why are the price breaks where they are?
What great ideas did marketing have when they packaged products in the way they did?

When you are discussing *ideas,* and approaches, it should reduce the customer's need to argue that another product is better.
Your customers will listen more acutely when you begin with something like:

Our engineers studied the application, and concluded that **these things** are most important and helpful to you. Our idea was to develop a product that would help you most if it...

The president of a company that distributed the products made by my employer, told me that he just couldn't sell our stuff. His reasoning was that a competitor was too firmly entrenched for him to get a fair shot. He had waited too long.
We talked for a while, and I asked him why he had decided to sell our products in the first place.
He told me, and reminded himself, that he saw lots of business potential, all going to one manufacturer, and he wanted a piece of it. Furthermore, he said that he had customers that wished they could

buy this competitive product from him. When he tried to get the line, he couldn't, so he looked into other solutions. He was initially enthusiastic about selling our products, because he saw them as better, cheaper, and that he could provide superior support than the competition.

However, he said, they just won't listen to me. They want to stick with what they have, and everybody around here has them.

My hunch was that his presentation was focused around what was better about his new product, compared to brand X.
*He was ending up in a place that was worse than when he started. Where he wanted to convince them that his product was **different better,** they defended their decision, and so they saw it as **different wrong.***

Take a moment and consider this behavior.
What people invest in is important to them. They are careful in their decisions, and are usually proud of their decisions and accomplishments. They have developed their beliefs, and they are not fools for buying something that you don't sell.
We generally don't like to be called fools, no matter how subtle it is. Everything that we own and we love, we can present reasons for. We know how we arrived at our passionate belief in it. We will defend these beliefs, if necessary.

As a completely unrelated example, I like what I like, just like everyone else. One of the things that I like is Irish whiskey. I prefer a particular brand and type, and have done a lot of "research" on the topic in the last thirty years.
Once, I was in a tavern. I was sitting next to a man that was about to tell me all about the fact that he preferred Scotch whisky. When the barman brought a bottle of Irish whiskey to me for a pour, he said, "You really like that crap? You should drink Scotch, it's a lot better."
For the next ten minutes, I defended my whiskey and knocked his. I shared my extensive knowledge and experience on the subject with him.
If he really wanted me to consider something new, he should try something other than insulting me.
Get the point?

That's what I believed was happening with this distributor. Although he would tell you that he would never insult a prospect or customer, he just might have been. At the very least, he was getting them to tell him how great the product was that he wanted them to move away from.

I made this suggestion.
See if you can get ten or twenty customers to come by to learn about your new products. Be sure to include the biggest users of the competitive products.
I'll come out, and make a presentation to each of them, that will include a product demonstration. When he told me that he could do a damn fine product demonstration on his own. I said fine, as long as I could make my presentation first.

Then, I went to work. I thought about what I wanted to say, and keep it to ten or fifteen minutes.
I knew that my customer was actually the distributor, not the end user, and I hoped to show him a different approach.
I spent hours making notes, and word smithing my presentation. I presented it to the dog, the mirror, and to myself, over and over, until I felt prepared.

The presentation started in this way.

*" I know that you are a user of brand X. They are a competitor of ours all across the country, and so I am familiar with their product. Today, I would like to tell you about **our ideas.**"*

*Then I outlined what we thought was most important to the **user** of the product. I went on about technology being useless if it seems too complicated to embrace. I listed five things that we thought were most important to **them,** which they nearly always agreed with. I introduced the ideas until I could say, "And so our idea was to develop a product that was better in each of these areas. Of course, in order for it to be better, it was often different from what you know. And John here can show you what we came up with."*
When these people went through the demo, they were intrigued to see if they could find something better than what they had, and they often did.
It was a successful day for everyone.

It was my goal that the distributor would keep the line. I needed a way to show him that another approach might be more helpful. Knowing that I only had one chance for success, I tried to put myself precisely into what his most difficult situation was. I then developed a presentation that I was confident would be thoughtful and persuasive. I worked on it for more than ten hours in a two-week time span.

At the end of that day of presentations, I felt that all of the preparation time was time well spent.
Over dinner, John told me, in different words, that I had created a compelling vision that he could believe in, and follow.
Sometimes, I am slightly less magnificent, as in the following shamefully true example.

A customer at a trade show was explaining to a salesman why he was going to buy a competitive product. He went on and on about what a great product and company it was.

I said, "They have done nothing to their product in the last ten years, except to raise the price. I guess that's why they went chapter 11 last week."

If you were guessing that the customer said, "Golly, aren't I just a misinformed moron. Thank you for enlightening me. Can I please buy something from you?"
Well, it wasn't like that at all. At least he let me apologize on his way out.

There was a point that I wanted to make, and the chapter 11 thing was true. I refined my presentation until it sounded more like this.

"It's true that they have earned a reputation for quality over many years. No one can doubt that.
However, it is also true that they have not made a significant improvement to that product in over ten years.
The customers that have chosen to buy a similar product from us often do so because they recognize that we try to offer real product improvements, and keep our price far below theirs. Others have done this also. That is probably the cause for their recent need to

reorganize financially. It's just not good enough to build a great product, and then rest on your laurels."

All true, slightly more effective. Example 1 was a display of me when I try to wing it. Example 2 is a refined and rehearsed presentation on a particular product or idea.

If you think that your presentations are clean and smooth, then I challenge you to try this.
Think of any single topic or question, on which you will certainly need to make a presentation. Pick something reasonable, but not the kind of thing that comes up every day.
Record your presentation, using a recorder or video camera. Say it just like you would say it to a customer. Then listen to it, over and over. Count how many times you say "um," repeat yourself, or just ramble on. Critique it to see if you accomplished what you set out to accomplish. If you find any need for improvement, try this:

1. Write down a name for this presentation. Does it present a thought, answer a question, or add clarity to a topic? Do this for any instance in which you are going to string more than three sentences together.
2. Jot down five or six points (maximum) that are important. After you have the list, prioritize them.
3. Wordsmith it. Practice it over and over, coming up with the most powerful and clear words and sentences that you can.
4. Offer a conclusion, when appropriate, and necessary.

On the other hand, you can wing it.

Discovery

From the very beginning of our life, we are taught, and we begin to learn.
When my children were little, I would watch them take anything small, and put it into their mouth, just in case it was food. When it wasn't food, they spit it out. They were discovering what is edible, and what isn't.

When my son was young, he would sometimes come too close to the wood stove. I would put my hand near it, and say "Hot!" Then he would put his hand in the air, mimic me, and say, "Hot!"
I tried putting my hand nearer to the stove, retract it quickly with a look of surprise on my face, and saying, "Hot!"

I was teaching, or trying to teach him, what hot meant, without much success.

When I was paying close enough attention, he came nearer to the stove, until he could feel the heat and sense the danger. "Hot," he shouted.

He had learned, because he had discovered what hot meant.

There are some who believe that we only learn those things that we discover. Perhaps it is so.

In sales, I think of this discovery in this way:

Find a way to give the customer the closest possible experience of owning the product.

If you don't think this works, contact your nearest crack cocaine vendor. You won't get a wordy description, or a snazzy brochure. You will get a taste. And then, you will know.

(Note. I am not advocating the use of crack cocaine or the sale or distribution of it. I have never used or sold crack cocaine. In fact, I think it is a very bad idea. Still, I think it is a powerful example, and it seems to work here.)

How else do we *know* something, unless we experience it?

So often, we seem to be offering words that are not unlike hearsay, or theoretical examples. They seem to make sense, but not enough for some action or change to occur.

Consider, for example, the idea of "User friendly." We know the intent of the message. We also know that no one describes their product as "User hostile," or "Too difficult for some people, maybe even you."

33

"User friendly," is a hollow description. What we need to know is this, "How easy will it be for me to use?" Right?

I know that pharmaceutical salesman often give away samples of drugs. Certainly, they could provide stacks of technical information, and they do. But why would they give away the product, unless it was to help doctors discover the effect on patients?

Clarence was selling, in the view of his manager, less than he could. Clarence was satisfied with his results. The manager believed that there was a strong correlation between Clarence's sales, and his low number of product demonstrations. I was asked to offer some help.

Clarence was clear in saying that he frequently offered product demonstrations, but that often people weren't interested, or didn't have time. He was also quick to point out that there were cases when he would explain how easy his products were to use, and would give examples of how the software worked, and customers were able to understand, accept, and buy.

*We talked for a while about how different people understood things in different ways. In point of fact, we all understand things in our **own way**.*

In our conversation, Clarence let me know that he was considering the purchase of a palm pilot type product. He let me know that he was quite savvy with high-tech products, and that he was researching different types, and capabilities.
I asked him if there was somewhere that he could try different types, and he said there was. My suggestion was that he go and do just that, to see if it made his decision any easier.
He did, and it did.

Clarence told me that he had resisted this, because he didn't want to have to go through endless application demos, about stuff that he was not interested in, or already understood.
So, he sort of took charge of his time with the salesman, learned what he wanted, tried out the applications that he was interested in, and decided on a product to buy.

Making the same point about his own customers was quite simple. In fact, he made it without any help from me.

The change that Clarence made was this: When he got a sense that the customer didn't really understand how easy his products were to use and learn, he would take a simple example that applied directly to them, and show them a very brief product demonstration on just that one thing. In most cases, it leads to the customer asking a lot of "Show me how it would…" questions.

So what happened? By working with Clarence about how he discovered things, it was easier for him to help others to really experience and discover how his products worked. He gave up on his previous belief of, "I told them, and it's so easy they should get it."

Helping customers to discover something, takes some patience. It requires that you understand precisely what they know, on some level, but cannot **value** experientially.

A customer had put off a decision several times to purchase a piece of equipment, because he was unsure of its strength. What he meant by strength was unclear to the salesman that had called me to ask for advice.
He told me that he had provided all of the technical data that should have satisfied this particularly picky prospect. The salesman said that the guy kept asking about "strength," but he didn't seem to really know what he meant by that, so how was he supposed to help him?
Since I often default to my mischievous, smart-aleck side, I suggested that he call the customer back, and explain to him what butterscotch tasted like, until he understood.
We wrangled a bit, until the salesman was frustrated enough to suggest that he would just "buy some damn butterscotch and put it in his mouth." This provided me with the opportunity to say, "My point exactly."

With the butterscotch out of the way, the salesman now saw the worth in making an arrangement whereby the customer could use the equipment, in exactly the way that he wanted to, and therefore provide him with a chance to experience and discover how *strong* it was.

Reduce the obstacle to this one issue:

When you are presenting an idea, or a concept, to people, sometimes the words are simply not enough. Even when a customer truthfully says that he understands, look for an understanding beyond some theoretical level.
It is your responsibility to provide something that will help the customer to discover, in their own unique way, how your product or service will be helpful, and be useable to them. And them alone.

Summary

1. Knowing your product and your industry are important. Study and memorize what is important to know. Set aside at least thirty minutes a day on these topics until you have reached expert status. After you are an expert, keep doing it.
2. Save your talking until you have the permission of the customer to hold forth.
3. Introduce product features and benefits that can be understood to directly improve the life of your customer.
4. Never introduce a solution, hoping that the customer has the right problem to suit it.
5. Practice, practice, practice your presentations. Continually refine them, based on the response of the customers.
6. Your words are your tools. Use them properly, and wisely. It is difficult to get a second chance to make a presentation. Customers won't grade you on your performance, or offer tips for improvement. They will nod, smile, thank you for your time, and then ignore you.
7.   Don't seize the opportunity to meet with a customer by telling him everything that you know. The only thing you will impress on them is that you stayed too long, obviously in love with the sound of your own voice. That makes it pretty hard to get the next appointment. They know what they are in for.
8. Customers, just like you and me, make the wrong choices for reasons that they think are right. No one intentionally makes a foolish decision. We just make uninformed decisions from time to time. Don't punish them for not knowing something by insulting them with a condescending attitude.
9. Be patient, we all need to discover things before we accept them.

I was a rookie salesman, my first week on the street with a new job. I was able to get in to see a guy that I believed would benefit from having our products.

He met me in the lobby, and welcomed me back to his office. I introduced myself as the new guy in the territory, and that we built a specific fabulous product, that he should have. I dumped every feature and benefit on him that I could recall from my training. I told him about the evolution of the product, and the important design features. I was at least ten minutes into it, when I noticed that he was holding the product in his hand.

I think that I stammered something glibly, like, "Where did you get that?"

He told me that they had 34 of them, and really liked them. In fact, he wanted to give me an order for four more.

Even getting my first order with my new employer didn't make the embarrassment go away. I had violated every rule of good selling, but hey, at least I got to talk a lot.

The next time I saw him, he was gracious enough to accept my apology.

I have always felt certain that if he were not already, because of the efforts of my employer, enjoying the benefits of the product, I would never have earned a chance to illustrate them.

Everyone would have been worse off, all because of my lousy selling skills.

Chapter 4

Do You Work Hard Enough?

Let's face it, working in sales isn't hard work, particularly if you compare it to lumber jacking, or coal mining. It has several perks that you really can't find in other jobs.

1. You get to work independently, and unsupervised, a great deal of the time.
2. If you work in a factory or an office and your boss or the person next to you is a jerk, you still have to deal with them every day. If a customer is really a jerk, you can leave, and never go back. (There are a few jerks, but not many.)
3. If you want a raise, just sell something. If you want another raise tomorrow, go sell something.

However, there are a few negatives in the life of sales.

1. Customers will often act indifferent to you, until they get to know you. They feel that is okay to be rude, and to tell us lies, just like we do to phone solicitors.
2. If you report every day to an office or factory job, all you have to do is show up and someone will give you work to do. Sales people have to create their own plan and itinerary. We have to create our own opportunities.
3. No sales=No money.

Unfortunately, many people see the life of a salesman as an easy one, skipping around from place to place and talking.

When my daughter was about eight years old, she asked me what I did for a living. I told her I was a salesman, and what I sold, to which she said, "But what do you do?"

I explained that I would go see a man at his office, and talk to him about things that would help him in his business. If they helped enough, he would buy them.

"What do you do after that?" She asked.

I explained that I would go see another man at his office, and talk to him about things that would help him in his business. If they helped enough, he would buy them.
"Then what?"

I said that I would go see another man at his office, and talk to him about things that would help him in his business. If they helped enough, he would buy them.

"That's all you do?"

It does sound kind of mundane, given that explanation doesn't it?

Still, that is the life of a salesman. Every sales opportunity is the same, and every one is different.

Some salesmen get so bored by this, that they slowly stop working. This happens most often with the salesman that is so lazy in his approach that he says the same things to everyone, and the ones that don't respond positively he gives up on, with the belief that he did all that he could.

Every customer is different from the one before him. Of course, there are certain classifications, types, and groups. However, every customer is different by virtue of his or her humanity. An important part of the work that a salesman has to do, is to tailor each sales opportunity to the individual that he is working with. This is hard work, from the standpoint of preparing for each call, but is necessary for success.

I was giving a sales seminar for a small group of salesmen and their manager. The topic was "understanding customers in a variety of ways."
It included discussions such as, how do they view challenges, what kind of buyer are they, how do they view taking a risk, what motivated them, and so on.
At the end of a rather grueling day, everyone seemed to agree that knowing a lot more about their individual customers would bring great rewards. One salesman, who didn't last too long in the world of sales, said, "This seems like a lot that you have to know, just to sell something to somebody."
The boss looked him right in the eyes and asked, "You mean you won't do something just because it's hard?"
"No, no, of course not" the man said.

Nevertheless, we all knew that was exactly what he meant.

I often talk about the few and precious hours that are available to us to do our work. Some call them the "Golden Hours." Not a bad description.

Every single solitary salesman that was successful *over the length of his career* had one thing in common. They worked hard, when they could.

What I mean by that is they used all of the selling time available, for selling. They weren't sitting in an office reviewing notes at ten in the morning. They weren't catching up on paperwork when customers were available to be seen, or to be called on the phone. Every single task that can be done away from customers should be done when customers are not available to be seen.

One of the most successful salesman that I have ever known works from his home office. At the end of the sales day, when he returns home, he goes directly to his office. Any paperwork that has to be completed is done then. When that is completed, the day is over, and he shuts the office door. The next morning he is back on the street, using his time to its best advantage.

Some may argue with me about the necessity of making notes immediately after every call, saying that it is best to save that task for the end of the day.

Well, that's just crap. Create an efficient system and it won't take long, no more than a few minutes. Writing it down when it's fresh and accurate is the only dependable way.

Denny is a great salesman. He sells a highly competitive commodity product that is differentiated only by price, delivery, and the salesman. I once asked what his secret was. He answered quickly. "The early bird gets the worm. I'm out there every day, and I am always the first salesman at my first call, sometimes even the second or third."

He means it too. I once was out with him till the wee hours, enjoying ourselves after a sporting event. I called him the next morning ay 6:30. He was already on the move for a 7:00 A.M. call. I wasn't.

Point taken.

Most companies divide sales territories up pretty closely by geography and potential.

At sales seminars, I always ask this question. "If the products are the same, the prices are the same, and the potential is about the same, why are results so different from one territory to another?"

Inevitably, the discovery is that the salesman is the only thing that is different, and it must have something to do with how hard he works. Generally, there are few that are shamefaced.

I asked Jim what he owed his success to. His answer was, as I expected, thoughtful. I had met Jim when I was a buyer, and he was the salesman that solved my problems. I know for sure that a part of his answer was that he always made a call after 4:30. He said that it kept him motivated when customers would invariably comment on how late he was working. He always told them the same thing. "Well, I figure that if you're working I should be working too."

Clearly is it easy to gain a competitive edge, when so many customers are surprised to see salesman working at 7:00 A.M., or 5:00 P.M., just like they are.

What does that say about most salesmen?

Roy had a big territory. It was easy for him to drive two hours or more from home to make a call. Every day, he would start close to home, and work his way to the outermost part of his territory. He felt entitled to a one-hour lunch, because that's what he got when he worked in inside sales. Every day, Roy arrived home at 5 P.M. If he was two hours way at three o'clock, he headed home.

"I give them their eight hours, that's all they're paying me for," he reasoned.

When he gave up sales, it was because it was too hard to live on the small commission that he earned.

Sales is a highly results-oriented career. They don't pay you for making calls; they pay you for making an impact. The more impact that you make, the more frequently you sell something. The more frequently you sell something, the bigger the paycheck.

It's a great job for hard-working people. A pretty tough one for the rest.

I was once told that it doesn't matter if someone can't pay you, or won't pay you. Either way, you don't have the money.
In the same way, he continued, if something doesn't get done, it's because you can't do it, or won't do it.

When I apply this to the things that I am not accomplishing, I change the verbiage a little. I ask myself the question, "Am I being stupid, or am I being lazy?"

Is it just too hard for me, or am I not trying hard enough? Are there things that I need to learn? Is there some bitter task that I am avoiding?

I have come to learn that in sales, it is not only how much you know, and it is not how many calls that you make.

I know plenty of salesmen that have way more technical knowledge about their products than I do, and don't sell a lot. That is because they have not worked hard enough at practicing their presentations, or mastered the art of shutting up, and learning what is important to the one and only prospect that they are talking to right now.

Lots of salesmen burn up the miles, and wear out their shoes, making hundreds of calls. However, they have not worked hard enough at creating an organized system to chart progress, and they have depended on volume of calls to make a difference, rather than making an impact on every call.

It comes down to the number of **good** calls that you make. That, and nothing else.

Your work ethic will define everything. It will define, most importantly; you will work hard enough to do:
1. Whatever it takes, whatever it is.

2. The critical work necessary to constantly and continually review the weakest of the nine areas (and other areas that you define) and get to work strengthening them.

Looking at the topic of work ethic from the negative side, here is an example of a salesman that wasn't working hard enough, on the correct things, to sustain a successful career in selling.

Mickey was a hard worker. By that, I mean that whatever he was working on, he gave it all the effort he could. He had spent a lot of time in his youth as a builder, and sweat was no problem for him. In sales, he got average results.

He understood that guys like him expected others around them to work hard. In his business, sales calls could often be made as early as 6:00 A.M., and he was always on his way by 5:30 in the morning. He had asked me to spend some time with him, as he had a dilemma that he did not know how to solve.

It was easy to see that those who liked and trusted Mickey did so completely. Whenever we went to see a customer, there was plenty of Mickey's equipment in use. However, in lots of other places, it was a big fat zero.

Mickey understood that there were lots of places with applications equal to the places where he had been quite successful.

I observed calls with both kinds of customers during the workday, and at the end of the day, we discussed things over a few beers. It is interesting to note that the place that he chose to meet, was a local tavern where everyone knew him, and that included several customers, and workers, who stopped to talk business with him.

I asked Mickey to figure out what was in common with the two groups of people. We labeled them as people who loved him, and people that didn't want to know him.

After some coaching, this is what he discovered.

1. His customers all seemed to be "regular Joe's" as he called them; hard-working guys, that were tradesmen. Most of his contact seemed to be with foremen and plant managers.

2. Mickey had a very "earthy," way of communicating. He was brash, funny, and sometimes quite crude. That was just his manner. I pointed that out to him, and he agreed.

3.   *I also pointed out that his presentations seemed to be the same, regardless of whom he was talking to. He explained that he had worked very hard to figure out "what worked," and he could point to the evidence to support his success.*

I asked Mickey what he thought of those prospects that he had seen that day that seemed to brush him off. He generally regarded them as "suits, that didn't know what went on in the factory."

It took a while for Mickey to discover that "what worked," worked very well with some people, but quite poorly for others. In the end, he discovered that he could only sell to people that he liked, and he didn't really like some of the people that he needed to do business with.

Mickey began to accept that he would have to either find a lot more customers in one category, or change his ways with the others. He was initially enthusiastic about getting some help, but his interest in learning and changing waned. He seemed to hold on to the idea of selling more to his current customers, and finding more like them. I recall clearly him making the comment, "I am what I am, and I can't be a chameleon."

After a while, Mickey's efforts and his results returned to where he had started.

Was it that he couldn't improve, or that he wouldn't improve?

Remember, he was a very hard working guy that I enjoyed being around, as did some other people.
Nevertheless, your work ethic has to include the ability to be smart about what deserves your attention for improvement.

Chapter 5

Do You Know Enough About Your Products
and The Industry That You Work in?

Tom was one of those glib, happy-go-lucky types of salesmen. Once he told me that he thought that he could sell anything to anybody. I had hired him based mostly on the fact that he had done pretty well for a few years as a competitor.

I spent a day in the field with him, a few months after he had completed his initial product training. On a particular sales call, he was to demonstrate a product for a customer. He rushed through the demonstration, providing only the most fundamental capabilities of the product.

Whenever a specific question was asked, he deflected it, making bold and hollow claims, like; "This product blows away all of the others in the field," and "Your people will love it, and want more." When asked for some comparisons to competitive products, he was equally bold and hollow, trash mouthing the competition. Some claims that he made were a little distant from the truth.

When we left the call, I was prepared to discuss his weaknesses in product and industry knowledge. I decided not to bother when he went on and on about how well it went, and how certain of a sale he was. I was pretty mystified by our contrasting perspectives.

I noticed in several other calls that day that he replaced facts with bluster. The look on the faces of the customers suggested that they didn't have much confidence in him, although he was fully unaware of this.

His career with this particular employer was over within six months. He really hadn't created many opportunities, or any impact, although he felt sure that customers would buy, because they liked him. In the six months that he had the job, he wrote no business that was not really created for him by the product itself, the company, or the previous salesman, who had been promoted from his territory.

I contacted the customer directly that I had observed the product demonstration on, shortly after his demise. I thought that there was plenty of potential for our products there.

"We are interested in the product," I was told, "But that salesman is a buffoon."

It is my opinion that there are three basic components to a sales job. By that, I mean you can divide up the requisite skills, into three "master" areas, to consider your competency. Your weakest area will be the biggest roadblock to sales. In no particular order, one area is selling skills, one area is product knowledge, and the other is industry knowledge.

Product Knowledge, is knowing all of the fine details about your own products. Please note that I am saying that you should *know* all of the technical details of the products that you sell, and how they work. Please don't think that I mean that you should fascinate your customers with your product wizardry. If you know everything about your product, you will be able to answer questions that are important to the customer.

Product knowledge means being able to use your own products. (If this is possible. I don't suggest this if you sell pharmaceuticals) and certainly you should know the specific and exact *effect* that your products have.

You should know why a product is the way it is.

There will, without doubt, be times that you will not be able to answer specific questions. That is understandable. But certainly there should not be half a dozen times that you say "I'll have to check on that and get back to you," in a single call or presentation. By the way, every time that you do promise to check something out and get back to the customer, I recommend that you get to work on that immediately following the call. If you can get back to the customer within an hour, that's great. Anything more than a day makes you appear to be lazy.

I mentioned *effect* earlier. This is as important as the actual science, or design of your product. For example, if you sell equipment, it is important to be able to discuss fluently the effect that the product will have on the life of the customer.

Since customers purchase equipment to solve or alleviate problems, then it is important to understand how **well** it will do this. This is the effect of the product.

In American business today, an important task for managers is to reduce the payroll.

That means making people more efficient, and accomplishing more, with less staff. As some CEO's and CFO's are prone to say, "If I buy this, who do I get to fire?"

That's not caustic, that is reality. American workers, and the way of life that we demand for ourselves, are expensive.

Be prepared to differentiate the cost of a product from its price, just as accountants and program managers do.

How much time will the product save, and what is the effect of the saved time? Armor yourself with specific product knowledge so that you can define your product, use your product, and define the value of the product.

Remember, if you don't properly value your product, your customers will apply their own value to it. The customer is less likely to be an expert than you should be. Being an expert on your own products should be your goal. If you study it, for thirty minutes every day, you will get there. Your fine selling skills will help you talk about the salient points of your product, instead of boring customers with your endless knowledge.

Don't worry about the questions that they don't ask. They will, if it becomes important. Important to them, that is.

Industry Knowledge is different from product knowledge, and is in some ways harder to acquire. One of the important parts of industry knowledge is knowing the lingo. If you sell printing presses or computers, hang around with the people that design, build and repair them, and you will hear phrases, words, and slang expressions that are known and understood by everyone in the industry. You should too.

Industry knowledge is also knowing your competitors products. It is quite important that you are knowledgeable on competitive products. This might be difficult to learn, but the more that you know them, the more you will understand the strengths and drawbacks of your own products.

I had called Dick, a successful salesman in a distant part of the country, to ask him about a customer that he had success with, that was opening a factory in my sales territory.
After our business was done, we chatted for a while, and he told me that he had spent nearly all day using a new product, built by our biggest competitor. This surprised me to say the least.
"I lost an order recently, and the customer explained to me that he just saw this product as being better for him. When he gave me the details, I could see why. After he had it for a month or so, I asked him if I could spend time going over it, because knowing the

competition is important to me. He answered my questions and let me spend some time using it on my own."
" What did you think of it? " I asked.
"Well I can tell you this. I'll never lose another order to it, now that I understand it. I really couldn't say too much before, because the customer knew more about it than I did."

For me, as a salesman competing against the same products, that was a "WOW." I was so inspired by his dedication to accruing knowledge of competitive products that I began to do the same myself. You tend to remember when people impress you with their dedication. This happened in 1985, and I recall the lesson clearly, today.

Product knowledge also means having a thorough knowledge of the companies that you compete with, their history, and how they go about their business. It means getting to know all of the players in field, and reading all of the trade magazines.

It also means knowing the history, and the marketing plan, of your employer.

Oddly, this point is often completely overlooked by salesmen. Some will do all of the necessary research regarding the weaknesses of the plan and structure of the competition, but will not be too well versed on the plan and the history of their own company. In other cases, they assume that the potential customer knows all about them, so they don't bother discussing it.

I view this as a potentially big hazard, for two reasons:

1. In a time of so many failures, foreclosures, mergers, and acquisitions, it is difficult to keep up without a scorecard.
2. Perhaps your competitor is defining your company to customers, and he is incorrect, uninformed, or disingenuous. (I have heard that there are some salesmen that can be a little reckless with the truth.)

There are many cases, particularly when products are very similar; that the end choice comes down to one issue.

Who you buy from is important!

Certainly, the individual salesman can be important, but the more that products become the same, the less important the salesman is. If you don't think this is true, consider your own buying behavior when you purchase something like a refrigerator, a television, or even a car.
Are you really hanging on every word that the salesman says? Do you depend on him to be a fountain of statistics and facts?
I sure don't; in fact, I often avoid, and generally think that I should disregard salesmen in these cases. I prefer to figure it out for myself. (You know, like read about it.)

However, the company that I am buying from is *very* important to me.

What is their reputation? What about service? Are they solvent enough to be around for the life of the product?

Eugene had been calling on a customer for several years, hoping to get a shot the next time they needed a product. He felt confident that his solution was better, and cheaper, than the products that they had been purchasing from their current supplier, over and over, for years. He asked me for some advice, and in our conversation, it became clear that he had done a thorough job of explaining both the advantages of dealing with him, along with the product advantages. He was very knowledgeable about the competition's strengths and weaknesses in their products. He was stymied as to what else to do, so he just kept going back, asking for a chance that never seemed to come. He admitted to me that he had even challenged his contact about the wisdom of buying a product that did less, and cost more.

I asked him why he thought the customer would do such a foolish thing, and he had no answer.

I suggested that he try a fresh approach.

"When you want to know something, figure out exactly what you want to know, and then ask that exact question," was my advice.

On his next visit, he did exactly that. He reported that he first asked his contact if he thought his product was at least worth considering, and the customer had to agree that it was.

He then asked why he wouldn't even consider switching.

The customer explained that he simply felt comfortable with dealing with the same company that they always had. They had been in business for more than fifty years, and he was afraid to take a chance on a start-up company. He also added that a wrong decision would tend to make him look bad.

He said that he felt that his contact started to really listen to him, when he asked what upper management would think about the fact that a better, cheaper solution was available.

Eugene also added that his own employer had been in business for more than fifty years (this was unknown to the customer), was in great shape financially, (also unknown), and had developed significantly more product improvements in the last ten years, (also unknown).

With the help of his contact, a meeting was arranged with senior management, who agreed to give him a chance on the future. The potential customer also investigated Eugene's claims and found them to be true. They did some research as to Eugene's employer, and were confident enough to finally accept a proposal, which ended in new business for Eugene and his employer.

Who people buy from is important to them. A strong background of *Industry Knowledge* helps you to make informed decisions and suggestions to a customer.

One final thought on this topic. I am not encouraging you to bash the competition. I am encouraging you to know enough to provide facts that will assist them in their decisions.

There is a highly technical name that you may not be familiar with that describes salesmen that use negative competitive data too severely, or simply play fast and loose with the facts, assuming the customer doesn't know any better.

They are called bullshitters.

Chapter 6

Are You Listening? Do You Understand?

I have been asked the following question many times. Probably, more than any other.

What is the biggest overall problem that salesmen face?

Of course, there are many, and some of them we can't do much, or anything, about.

Often, I rephrase the question to say, "Do you mean what is the biggest problem that salesmen create for themselves?" I know the answer to that one.

They don't listen. Actually to be more accurate, and more specific, the problem is that they don't care to listen. This is because they want to use the time that they have with the customer to do the most important thing that they can think of. Talk.

Talk, talk, and talk.

Blah, blah, blah.

They want to tell the customer every potentially useful thing that they can think of, just in case it becomes important later. There is even the foolish expectation that the customer will remember all of the verbal vomit that they spew forth.

Perhaps I am being just a tad overzealous in my description, but I hope that it helps me to make a point. Salesmen talk too much, about the wrong stuff.

Some say that this poor habit keeps the salesmen in a zone of comfort. What if the customer got control of the conversation, and they asked a question that the salesman couldn't answer?

The great Dr. Steven Covey lists this as one his Seven Habits: (By the way, if you haven't read his work, you should be ashamed of yourself.)
<u>Seek First to Understand, and then to be Understood.</u>

If you are one of those irritating feature-dumping, content-telling sales types, than you probably also have a hard time getting repeat appointments with customers. This is because they know what they are in for on your visit. Another 45 minutes of you telling them what you know. How exciting.

Questions, good ones are the tools. The habit is to avoid trying to sell something to someone if you don't understand their problems, their situation, their circumstances, their challenges, and their obstacles.

Mark is a nice guy, well spoken, sincere, and educated. He came to me at the suggestion of his boss, because neither of them truly understood how a bright, hard-working guy like him could be such an ineffective salesman.

I can recall how sincere Mark was at solving this problem, much more so than many guys that are told by their boss to go and get help.

I asked Mark why he thought he wasn't selling, and he really didn't know. I asked him how important it was that he overcome this challenge, and he said that if he didn't improve, he would leave sales and return to engineering, which he didn't want to have to do.

I asked Mark if he could think of two or three selling situations where he was frustrated because he felt the customer needed his products, and would benefit from owning them, but he was unable to make progress. He had more than a few that he could cite instantly. I asked him to pick one, and tell me all that he could about the situation. His description was clear, and concise. I understood everything that he told me, just having to ask one or two questions to be certain that I understood what he meant.

Then, I began to ask Mark some questions. Questions that I needed to know the answers to, if I was going to be able to provide any kind of help.

I asked questions like these:

1. *Who will decide, and who can influence the purchase?*
2. *What problem do they need to solve?*

3. *How important is solving this problem? That is, what priority does it have?*
4. *How well does their current solution work, and what drawbacks does it have?*

Mark was fairly sheepish, as he answered, "I don't know," to each question.

The second example went pretty much the same way, and so we never bothered with the third.

I can recall asking Mark how much time he had spent with these two potential clients, and was surprised that he had spent as much time with them as he had. I presumed that this was because he was such an affable guy, with sincere intentions.
I was purposefully quiet, waiting to see what discoveries he had made during our brief interview. It's possible that I remember this entire conversation so well, because of what Mark said next.

"You could fill a thimble with what I know about these guys, huh."

A wise statement indeed.

I asked Mark if it would be okay if we stopped there for today, as we had been talking for more than thirty minutes. He said that he would prefer to know what I thought the problem was.

I said that I wanted to think about it, and would rather resume the discussion in a day or two. He acquiesced. The truth was that I wanted him to have time to think about it, which I knew he would do.

It was before 8:00 A.M. the next day, when Mark called. He started the discussion this way, obviously having given it a lot of thought.

"I really need to ask questions, don't I?"

"Yep. How did you discover that," I asked?

"I was embarrassed talking to you yesterday when I couldn't answer any of your questions. It really began to sink in last night, when you made me see how ineffective I am with customers. I was feeling

pretty good about all that I knew about my products, and that never even came up, when you and I talked. I kept thinking about you telling me I need to ask better questions, to know more about the customer's problems. Then I realized that you never told me one single thing. All you did was ask a few questions."

Mark was now ready to change his habit. Learning what questions to ask, and why was quite easy for him, and fun for us both.

If both you and your customer understand what he is really trying to accomplish, he will allow you to work with him on doing so. He will allow you to:

Provide Help

In the field of social work and psychology, a recurring definition of help consists of three parts. What I mean by this is; unless all three parts are in place, there is no genuine help. These are, *empathy, support, and reality.*
It is my belief that to help a customer, this is also true. I also believe that if you have a way to help him, he will be delighted to take ownership of your products and services.

Before delving into that, it is important for me to say that sales should be seen, in some ways, as a helping profession.
In this section, when listening is being discussed, it is important to remember that for any help to occur, you must listen to the customer so that you can understand what challenges he faces, and what he is trying to accomplish. If you understand this, and can offer a way to solve the problem, or at least alleviate it, you are helping him. Moreover, he will accept it. Your prospects and customers have no interest in helping you, but they will move heaven and earth to help themselves.

Howard was just getting started in business when I first met him. He was a real go-getter, and was anxious to make his mark in the world. Howard had big dreams. Of course, when he was starting out, his dreams outstretched his capital. He talked with me several times about the big and fancy equipment that he would buy one day. He was also clear in telling me that the equipment that I had to offer did not nearly match what he had in mind.

At that time, Howard was working out of a very small building, which certainly would not have housed the equipment that he had in mind. Nevertheless, dreams are not slaves to facts. Howard knew precisely what he wanted, and why, even though he did not have the space or the money to buy it. I believed him when he said that he would work 16 hours a day, doing things the hard way, until he could get what he wanted.

On my first several visits with Howard, I realized that I was heading in exactly the wrong direction. The more that I tried to tell him about my products, the more he was able to stiffen his resolve about what their drawbacks were, and why they were wrong for him.

I would like to point out that if in your sales work you are convincing your prospects how wrong your products are for them, that this is a bad idea.

On my next visit to Howard, I asked him if I could propose an idea to him. First, I let him know that I understood that I could not offer the products of his dreams, just so that he didn't take any more time convincing me. Then I pointed out that for about one third of the money, he could get two thirds of what he wanted. In addition, he could probably afford to do this now. He was intrigued enough with the idea that we spent a fair amount of time figuring out which solution got him the equipment of his dreams earlier. Would it be by working very hard with very limited capability, or by spending enough money on automation to reduce his manufacturing times?

The small investment made the most sense, in dollars and cents, by far. It didn't take Howard long to get the money together for a piece of equipment, and within a month he wanted another.

We had a good laugh, when after just a few weeks he was seeing big improvements. He laughed when he said, "Why didn't you make me do this before?"

As my job responsibilities changed, I lost track of Howard for about ten years. When I saw him at a trade show, we had a nice visit, and he showed me a brochure of his business, which, of course, included the building and equipment of his dreams, (along with two pieces of equipment that he had bought from me.)

Howard introduced me to his son, describing me as "a friend that helped get him started in business." He then told his son the story, just as I have told it to you here.

I recall how proud I felt, knowing that I had, in some small way, helped Howard to realize his dreams.

In this story, the nature of help came together for Howard and me. The empathy was the fact that I fully understood what he wanted, and why. The support was in the fact that I gave him a way to get where he wanted to go. The reality was when we calculated just how long it would take him to get there, using his present methods, compared to investing in equipment now.

When I sold this equipment to Howard, I got a commission. Twice in fact, and the second commission required virtually no work, other than to replicate his first order. Still, the return that Howard got on his investment far outstripped what I got.
But I did receive something far greater. Howard told lots of people that I was a salesman worth listening to.

Another tool that you are positioned to use, if you have listened to, and truly understand your customer, is that you learn how they view taking a risk. In Howard's case, he loved taking a risk. He proved this by quitting a good job to go out on his own. He proved it by investing in equipment very early in his career, and continually investing in this way, as he grew and grew, taking business from his competitor's and leaving them far behind.
Howard was the kind of guy that knew that he would be able to figure out newfangled technology along the way.
Certainly not everyone is like this, In fact, most are not. Many more of your customers are held back from progress, because of how they feel about taking a risk.
There have been many studies on this topic, including the work that The Sanford Research Institute did, called VALS grouping. I recommend this to you, for your study.

In basic terms, there is a full spectrum of folks that define the curve of risk taking.
On one end, are the people that are like Howard. On the other end, are the guys that seem to think that they have to wait until all of the lights are green, before they leave for town. (That is a Zig Ziglar expression that I love.)
One is not better than the other. It does you no good to judge people on this. The point is this:

The more that you understand folks; the more you will be able to help them.

Let me throw in a word of caution here. It has to do with intent, and manipulation. When I suggest that you understand people so that you can help them, it is *they* that deserve the help, not you. Of course, I am of the belief that the more people that you help to make money, the more that you deserve yourself.

Helping people by understanding them is not a parlor trick. It has to do with sincerity on your part, and your belief that what you offer them will be of benefit to them.

If you manipulate someone to get a sale, they may buy from you. But once they discover the manipulation, your relationship is over.

Anyway, back to risk. To paint it with the broadest possible strokes, people can be divided up into three different groups, with a thousand shades in between, regarding taking the risk that is necessary to invest.

Group One. The people that fear risk the most are best identified in two ways:

They are quite happy with things the way they are. Once they figure something out, they stick with it. They are not too adventurous, so they like to stay with their routine. They eat at the same restaurants, Thursday is meat loaf night, and they generally buy the same kind of plain car or truck over and over. They vacation in the same spots, and they use the same way of doing things, because that is what they know. When folks like this take the huge risk of going into business for themselves, it is a long, slow process. Often, they have a partner, to make the transition less, well, risky.

Group Two. The guys in the middle need to figure it out for themselves.

This group is often very conservative (thrifty) in their life style. A way of identifying them is that they don't like things like advertising or salesman, whom they don't trust to tell them the whole truth. So, they do lots of research, and reading, because they want to get the fine details. You probably have run across prospects that don't seem to keen on listening to you, but are interested in any data that you can provide. People like this enjoy spending hours on the Internet, researching any investment of more than twenty dollars.

Group Three. These people love a risk. They know that they are the ingredient that will make it work, whatever it is.
These types of people are generally early adopters of technology. They like to have all of the advantages, and they want them first. They will listen to a salesman's spiel, as long as it is interesting, which isn't generally for too long. Unlike group two; they will dismiss the importance of knowing every detail, because they are confident they will figure things out when they get there.
If I am correct about my divisions, then you should be able to assign yourself closely (not perfectly) within one of those groups.
Now that you can identify your prospect in a certain way, the question is: How do you help them?

Group One.

They need lots of assurance, and they like to know that everyone else in the world has already accepted the solution. The people in this group are late adopters of technology; they like to know that someone else has worked all of the bugs out.
When providing referrals, they only care about people like them, not big impressive corporations.
Another extremely important message to get to them is that there will be plenty of support to get them started.
By letting them know that many others, like them, have had success, and that there will be people that will help them ease into the change, the risks are minimized.

Group Two.

Basically, there are only two things to keep in mind here. The folks in this group don't mind change, and they often love technology. They just don't like glitz. Check out the cars that they drive; they are always sensible, spartan cars. No frills, no extras. Extras take away from the value, in their mind. They are prone to saying things like, "You don't need all that."
So keep things basic and factual, they endure sales people as little as possible. However, load them up with stuff to read. They are comfortable when they can do their own research.

They see risk as buying things you don't need, and taking someone else's word for it.

Group Three.

An interesting group. Whereas the guys in Group One like to know that everyone else has one, these guys always prefer to be first. They are willing to take a risk, to get an advantage over others. Don't bog them down with any details that they don't express interest in. Unlike Group Two, they tend to do enough research to get the basics, but then have confidence that they will figure things out along the way. Stick to real advantages, new things, which can keep them out in front.

I was on a sales call with Peter. The customer, by his conversation and demeanor suggested that he was in Group Two. The application for Peter's product was good, but the customer kept asking about anything more "basic."
Whenever Peter would offer to tell him more, he would begin reading the product literature. The customer agreed to think about it, and said he would call when he had made a decision. It was a frustrating call for Peter; he just never felt that he got very far, and doubted that the customer would ever call.
I suggested that Peter do this. "Stop back tomorrow with a complete product manual, and operating manual," I said. "Just tell him that you thought it might be helpful in making his decision."
Peter had a few other ideas, which I thought would be viewed by the customer as too pushy, and therefore manipulative.
"Check back in a few days," I recommended, "if you haven't heard from him. If he says that he read the manual, ask him if there are any questions that you can help him with. If he says that he read the manuals, you can ask for the order."
I knew that Peter wanted to do more, but he humored me, perhaps just to prove me wrong.
He called me in a few days to say that he had followed my suggestions. When he asked for the order, he got a quick yes.

Peter, being the strident student of sales that he is, then spent 45 minutes on the phone with me. His first question was, "How did you know that would work?"

My probably-too-lengthy answer included this comment:

People tell us who they are. They tell us what they like, and what they fear. They will communicate to us what motivates them, and what repulses them, if we just pay attention.

In addition, the more we understand them, the easier it is to help them.

The tool that sets the stage for listening is having the right questions.

In most cases, it is best to initially ask broad questions that will provide broad answers. These kinds of questions encourage the customer to respond freely, and provide you with an overview of their life, the circumstances, and the obstacles that the customer faces. They should also provide much needed information about the business that his business is in.

These would be questions that begin with words like:

- Can you tell me about…
- What is…
- I'd like to know more about…

These are the questions at the big end of the funnel. After a time, you should arrive at the small end of the funnel, wherein the customer clearly tells you about something that he would like some help with.

The funnel gets smaller by asking more direct questions, because you are listening acutely, and focusing on what the customer says, and what he means. If you are unclear as to what the customer means, ask him. Ask him with questions that begin with things like:

-Are you saying…
-If I understand correctly….

You will either be on the right track, or the customer will quickly put you back on it.

A technique that I always use for myself, I call a hinge. When a customer tells me something, I want my question to hinge off what he just said. That helps me to stay on the one and only topic that is important, and that is whatever the customer wants to tell me about. For instance, if a customer says, "I have been thinking that maybe I should look into the latest widget technology," you just might be prone to responding, "Our company is the best widget builder in the world, with the latest technology, and..." Complete the sentence with whatever verbal vomit you wish, because the customer will sense correctly that you have stopped listening to him.

You have learned very little with the "*I have been thinking that maybe I should look into the latest widget technology,*" comment. Keep your next question hinged to his statement. You might say:

Why are you thinking that?

What kinds of technology?

Can you tell me more about this?

If you adopt this habit, it may seem like you are missing the opportunity to lecture him on your wonderfulness, but it actually accomplishes two things:

1. It streamlines the conversation, because you are talking about the things that interest the customer.
    Just as importantly, if you do this well, you might learn that there is nothing that you can do to help solve his problems. That gets you out the door, without wasting time for you both.
2. It may give you an opportunity to understand a very specific goal on the part of the customer, which you have a solution for.

Remember, there is no sense in bringing up a solution, just in case the customer has a problem that matches it.

Good questioning and interviewing skills demonstrate a level of professionalism to prospects and customers, and it also demonstrates a level of courtesy that makes any conversation go more smoothly.

Here is an actual, and really bad example of poor listening skills, and just asking enough questions so that the salesman can rattle on.

I was interested in buying a wide screen T.V. The only thing that I really knew about them is that they seemed expensive.

As I was surveying the seemingly endless display models, mostly just comparing the prices, a salesman approached me.

Listen to his first question.

"How big you looking for?" He asked.
I didn't know, because my decision would be based more on price than size. So I said I wasn't sure.
So, he walked me over to a T.V. the size of a drive-in movie screen. "Way too big." I said.
So we walked to another T.V., still far too large, and stared at me. He, of course, didn't know that the room where I watch T.V. is fairly small. So he said, "You get something like this, and you get a couple of recliners, you can watch football all day Sunday."
Of course, he didn't know that the room won't fit two recliners, or that I hate recliners almost as much as I hate football.
I tried to interject a need of my own, when I began to get the lecture. It included words that were foreign and exotic to me. Words, like "pixels," and "High def," and "200 channels."

Because of my background and interest in selling conversations, I am always eager to make things easy for the sales person, although sometimes I am intrigued as to just how much their "salesmanship," becomes counter productive, or irritating.
" I'm not interested in channels at all," I said.
Of course, he didn't know that I never watch a T.V. station, and I only use a TV to watch DVDs.
He responded with some fascinating words about being cable ready, and that also, he had a crack team that would mount it on my wall, so that I didn't wreck my brand-new TV. That was followed by several engaging stories about great big expensive TV's that were installed improperly, and that you're just out of luck when that happens.

Of course, he didn't know that the room where the TV would go had only angled walls, so it could not be wall mounted.

I said, "We think that 36" is about as big as we could go," aiming to make a purchase in this century.

He remarked that my friends wouldn't think much of that, and that I wouldn't be able to have a Superbowl party. At least he laughed when he said that, so I laughed also.

It was difficult for him to walk me toward the teeny-weeny 36" TV's, but when we got there, he began to bore me again about hundreds of channels.

I just kind of stared into space, waiting until another customer would approach him. When another customer approached him, he walked them over to the gigantic TV. This gave me a chance to look around. When another salesman came by, I avoided eye contact, or grunted a "just looking," in their direction.

After a few minutes, I found something that I was interested in. I approached a different salesman, and asked him if the stand that the TV was cradled in was included in the price. He responded, "You really want to hang it on the wall. We can do that for you, because you don't want to take a chance on it falling down and breaking." I just looked at him until he finished, and when I was absolutely certain that he was done talking, I asked if the stand was included. He said it was.

Of course, he also didn't know that the room where the TV would go had only angled walls, so it could not be wall mounted.

Finally, I said, "I'll take that one, if you have one in stock, and I am not interested in an extended warranty of any kind."

He led me toward the register. On the way, the first "salesman" whispered something to him about my being "his" customer. So, the first guy took over. I had to be kind of curt, and cut him off about the warranty. As he was completing the sale, I told him that I needed to know if it was in stock. He kept going and said that even if it wasn't, he couldn't deliver for 3-5 days anyway.

I said that I was going to take it with me, and he said that it was better if it was delivered, and that delivery was only $35.00 anyway.

He went on to say that they were big and heavy, and expensive, and, it would have to wait for the installers to get there, and that could take 5-7 days.
When I learned that there were none in stock, I left.
My next stop went much more smoothly, and I bought a TV that I took home that day.
Driving home, and thinking about both examples, I was reminded of something that my friend Mike has said. It is a quote attributed to Attila the Hun.

"Every Hun has a purpose, even if it is to be a bad example."

Think about how little interest the salesman had in learning about what I wanted. He had certainly not developed the habit of seeking to understand. He had not developed any skills that enabled him to ask questions that would help him to help customers.

At least he did get to waste my time and his time. After my irritation wore off, I saw the whole thing as so comical that I have added it to my repertoire of "Things to Avoid."

Chapter 7

Can You Develop New Business?

Prospecting, suspecting, working with referrals, and getting started.

Marco was not too bad at selling overall. He made a good appearance and presentation, and was excellent at following through on the sales process. However, his days were very seldom long ones, and he never seemed to make it beyond the middle of the pack, performance-wise.

As his manager, I had trouble seeing why he wasn't selling more. So, I decided to ask him where he thought his roadblocks were. He knew, instantly.
"If a guy calls me up, or if I get a lead from a trade show or advertising, I really go after it, because I know they're interested. But I really suck at cold calls."
This was so glaringly true, that I don't see how I could have overlooked it. We went to work on it together, but he never really got over his disdain for prospecting and cold calling, which ultimately cost him his job.

Many, many salesmen are just like this. They seem to need too much permission from a customer in order to get the selling process started. They also assume that there is no need for their products or services, unless the customer enthusiastically greets them with open arms at the beginning of the process. They believe that because the customer is indifferent to their presence in their lobby, office, or on their phone, that they have no applications, challenges, or problems. The truth is, whether we like it or not, customers that don't know us are going to treat us with the same courtesy that we give to telemarketers at dinnertime. If the customer can get rid of you for life by giving you a "we're all set," or "I'll call you if I need you," then you may just be too wimpy to survive in the sales profession.

If, however, you are tough enough, here are some suggestions, tips, and techniques for getting started.

1. If you don't strengthen your skills in every area of your job, your weakest area will collapse your career like a house of cards. So it is with organization. In order to get to potential customers, you have to know who they are. You need to find a way to load your database with every prospect and suspect

in your territory. Most sales managers can provide you with the resources for finding suspects. Customer lists, phone books, ad leads, purchasing guides, the Internet, and so on. Your job is to get every one of them into the database, with some note about them being a suspect. Then, when you are planning to spend some time in a particular geography, their name will be in front of you, to make that initial phone call, or visit.

This data has to be present, and right in front of you for those days when three customers in a row cancel appointments, and the call that you allotted ninety minutes for, took nine.

Note where you are; look up those suspects by geography, and make that initial call. In case you forgot, all of that time building the database should be done outside of those few and precious selling hours that we get in a day.

2. Decide that you are going to go into business with this prospective customer (prospect, suspect) until you believe that it is no longer worth *your* time. If customers have a building and a sign on it that identifies that they are in business, we are entitled to go about *our business*, which is to walk into their door to see if working together will provide mutual benefit. View your very first call or visit to any customer, as the first step in a process that you will drive.

3. On that initial call or visit, only two potential things can happen. Either they will give you time, or they won't. I am going to assume that you know perfectly good and well what to do if someone says, "Sure, I have a few minutes," or "If you can have a seat, he'll be with you shortly." As you know, these are rare, so you need to be prepared for indifference.

Kenny was on a field workday with his boss. They sat together in a lobby, making a cold call on a customer that seemed would have great potential for their products. They were second in line behind another salesman. The gatekeeper, a grizzled, mean looking woman that seemed to take delight in running salesmen out of the lobby, summoned him to the window by crooking her long and bony index finger.

" I'd like to see the purchasing agent please," said the salesman. "About what?" She asked, with a wicked half smile. "We sell, blah, blah, blah," responded the salesman, looking weak in the knees. "Leave some literature and I'll pass it along," said the wicked witch. The salesman then unloaded more product literature on her than any purchasing agent would read in a year. As he turned to leave, he looked at Kenny and said, under his breath, "Good luck."

"Who's next?" she boomed, in a caustic, uninviting way. Kenny strode to her, with only a business card in hand. "Ma'am, I've never been here before and I need some help." He paused, waiting for a response that never came. "You see, we build widgets, and I am not sure who I would meet with. Usually I talk to the plant manager or a foreman."

"That would be Mr. Smith, but he only sees salesman by appointment."

"Does he set his own appointments, or a secretary?" Kenny inquired. "He does."

"Okay" Kenny said, and took a moment to write something on the back of his business card. "Would you give this to him? On the back it says that I will call him Friday, to set up an appointment for next week." The gatekeeper agreed, unsure if she had put another notch in her belt or not. Kenny did call Friday, and he did get an appointment, which got him into the door of what would one day become his biggest customer. On the way to the car, the manager made the following comment.

"People that greet or see salesmen for a living assume that out of one hundred people that darken their door, about three of them will be worth anything to them. The salesman before you is one of the ninety-seven. He'll never go back unless they call, and he wasted fifty bucks in literature. You are one of the three percent."

If you decide to see a customer, see it as the beginning of a process that you are responsible for driving. You have decided to talk to the customer to see if there is potential gain for you two getting to know each other. The customer doesn't need to agree with this. You should be willing to accept that they cannot, or will not, give you some time now, because you have stopped in unannounced. However, that is the only thing that you should accept. You went to see them for a reason. Stay on it until you are convinced there is no application. If it takes ten visits and twenty phone calls, then that's what it takes. Just keep I mind that the other ninety seven percent will give up before you do. Be mindful that one of things that can set you apart from all others is your willingness to give your word and keep your word. Every call needs a plan of action. Tell them what you are going to do next, and do it. If you say you are going to call Friday to make an appointment, then make a note that you are going to, and follow through.

You get to start slightly up the ladder by saying; "I was in your lobby last Tuesday. I left my card with a note saying that I would call you today for an appointment, to see if you might have an application for our products. How is next Wednesday for you?"

4. Some guys just don't like cold calling. If that is the case with you, I am offering a technique for getting calls by referral, which has proven to be quite successful. Here goes:

It is important that you use this technique at the right time. It is based loosely on the Law of Reciprocity, which means that people are willing to give to people that have given to them. Therefore, this needs to begin after you are certain that you have done something of value and worth for a customer. Generally, but not always, this will be after the customer has begun enjoying the considerable advantages that your product has delivered, just as you promised.

When the time is right, you tell the customer that you would like to ask him for a favor. You might provide some explanation as to why you are looking for his help. The best thing to tell him is the truth. Let him know that getting in the door at places is difficult for a salesman. Remind him that most guys are just too busy to take time away from the important tasks of their day to talk to yet another peddler. After that, these are the exact words that I recommend you say:

" I was hoping that you could provide me with the name of one friend of yours that would benefit from owning our products." That's it. There is no manipulation here, you are asking for help. You are asking for the name of a friend, because the people that he has a relationship with are important to him. We are inclined to help our friends.

If you have done a good job, he will say yes. If he thinks that putting you in touch with people he cares about will make him look bad, he won't. He won't offer to put you in touch with anyone that he wouldn't want to give an advantage to, such as an enemy or a competitor. However, I'll bet he has one name for you.

When he provides the information, make sure that he sees you writing it down, so that he sees that you value it. He will have all of the pertinent data in his head, or at his fingertips. He will probably tell you how to get there.

When I was a salesman in the field, I found this to be so helpful that it provided all of the new account business I could handle. In many cases, I had already seen, or had tried to see, the name that he gave me. Sometimes I would ask if he would write something like, "Dave, you should see this guy," and sign his name on a business card. Many times, he would offer to call him, as I was sitting there. One guy even took me there!
At the very least, you will be starting a few rungs up the ladder if you can say, "Your friend Dave over at ABC Corp. suggested that I talk you about a product that he thinks would help you."

More times than not, even though I clearly asked for just one referral, I got several. This really helped me to get inside a community that my customers belonged to.

One other thing. It is my suggestion that after you follow through, you express your gratitude for providing the referral.

A wise man once told me, "Business isn't business, like people say. Business is personal. We want to do business with people we know and trust."

Opportunities and Impact

A rookie salesman bragged to his boss, "I made 22 calls today. I would have made a few more, but somebody asked me what I was selling."

I once got into a bitter argument with a high level sales manager. The manager was chiding me, because he felt that my critique of the new salesman was going to demotivate him. The salesman had reported to the high level manager, correctly, that I told him that making a lot of calls was of no value, if you weren't making a difference. The high level manager told me that the salesman was working hard, and he didn't want that disturbed. He is still wrong, and I am still right.

It is true that salesmen need to work hard, and it is true that they need to be motivated in order to do well. It is my contention, however, that nothing becomes more demotivating than making call, after call, after call, and never really getting anywhere. After a while, if he is poorly managed and directed, the salesman will get the message that going to a lot of places is good, and so that is all that he does. He accepts that everyone is too busy, or not interested. For a weeks, maybe longer, the salesman may cheerily go on knocking on doors, but in time his pace will slow and his interest will wane, as he discovers just how pointless this job is.

To be clear, I think that it is important for a salesman to work hard, but he has to work hard at creating opportunities, and making an impact with prospects. It's about the quality of calls, along with quantity.
If the best that you can do on the first call is to validate your belief that there is an application for your products; that's okay. Then you need to know whom you should be meeting with, then you need to know when you can have that meeting, then you want to learn about the customers' challenges, while you introduce your products.
Look for an opportunity for your products, and then get prepared to make a presentation.
On each of these steps, take a businesslike approach so that you are creating an impact.

What is the difference between what I'm recommending, and just being satisfied by showing up at a lot of places?

Primarily, it is your mindset. Prepare to make progress, and be disappointed, rather than satisfied, when you don't.

All of this goes back to my argument with the high-level sales manager.

Starting off in a new sales job, or beginning your career in sales, is tough work. It takes persistence. Many salesmen start off a new job doing their best to hide their inexperience, or their lack of product knowledge.

However, nothing will deflate a salesperson more than accomplishing nothing. If you begin with the idea that you are creating a process, and looking for opportunities, then you will, at least some of the time. Tomorrow you can do a little better. Next week you might be seeing a customer for the second time, and really begin to feel as though you are getting somewhere.

That is what should motivate you.

Begin a process, create opportunities, and make an impact.

Keep in mind that sales people don't get paid for making calls. We get paid when we make a difference.

Summary.

1. Plan to spend a certain amount of time every week, getting started with new customers. Don't wait until you have bugged every other customer to death that has hinted at some interest, to start the process with new prospects. Make it something that you allot an appropriate amount of time to.
2. Be organized in your database to see new customers when you find unexpected time to do so.
3. Be prepared to do business on every call. Expect that a customer will see you, and you will be prepared when they do. At the minimum, you want to establish that you are beginning a process, not just, "stopping by because you were in the area."
4. Always be mindful that if you don't create some impact from the beginning, it will be the same as if you were never there.
5. Use your established relationships to create new ones, through referrals.

Chapter 8

Can You Keep The Process Moving?

Closing (and why it is good)

You may have heard me say, as many have, many times, that every call needs to be closed. In every step of the sales process, each and every call needs to be closed. This means that:

- Both parties agree on the next step
- It is clear as to any work that will be done, and by whom.

Each facet is equally important.
In the next section, we are discussing the most rewarding and fun kind of closing, the kind when you win the business.

There are three kinds of closers:

1. The ABC guy. If you haven't heard it before, it stands for "Always Be Closing." Far be it from me to ever say that trying to make the sale is bad, but the point that I wish to make here is that attempting to close a sale at the wrong time can become a negative. I was once told that customers figure out in just a few minutes if you are there for *your* benefit or for *theirs.* Asking for business that you haven't earned can make you appear to be a peddler. Do you want to look like a peddler?
2. The guy who is afraid to close. Some salesmen really don't want to ask for the order, because the customer might say no, and then they will shrivel up and die. They will have no idea what to say, and so they will probably begin to cry. To a lesser extreme, some salesmen are afraid to ask for the order, because they think the customer is "not ready." I guess they have some sort of sales Ouija board that will tell them when the planets are aligned correctly for them to timidly ask for permission to ask for the order. These types often use what they call a trial close. Trial closes are not real. They are a bad idea, and some sort of trick that some guy thought up to sell books.
3. Real businessmen.
The very best (the guys with the most orders, the richest guys) salesmen understand that they function as an unpaid consultant to their customers. They think of the investment that the customer

needs to make as if it is their own money. They also understand that it is their *responsibility* to recommend the course of action that the customer takes, and to tell them why. All throughout the selling process, they have demonstrated to the prospect that he has their best interest in mind.

That is why they have asked so many questions. That is why they have dealt with customer misconceptions and skepticism. They have found the necessary ways to help the customer fully understand the benefit and impact of their products and/or services.

Frank had called for an appointment, saying that he wanted to stop in and go over a few details. He was clear in saying that he thought that a decision on their part should be imminent. During the call, Frank was surprised that the customer indicated that they were ready to make a purchase that was three times greater in price than the solution that Frank had in mind. It was also clear to Frank that they were making the wrong choice. When he asked them how they had arrived at their decision, they felt that having less technology in many locations would be superior to adding more (appropriate) technology to only one work area. They stated that this would give them the best "bang for their buck." They understood that they would be less capable, but they would be adding something, in more places.

I was impressed when I heard Frank say the words, " I disagree. Here is what I would do if it was my money."
I could see the surprise on the face of the customers.
Frank explained that if they bought more technology in one place, it would have a greater impact. He backed it up with numbers, and also reminded them of a few capabilities that they would not be getting, that they had told him were important earlier in the sales process.
He continued that if they bought the wrong technology; they would eventually discard it when the results proved to be unsatisfactory.
I watched with amusement, when the customers reminded Frank that he was asking them to spend less money than they intended to.
Frank responded in two ways. First, he said that he just would not be doing his job if he allowed them to invest poorly, even if it

meant more money for him. Secondly, he told them that if he was right, the chances are that they would use this technology in many places, once they understood the impact that it would make.
They then said something that I found as interesting as Frank's response to it.

" It's a budget thing Frank. If we don't spend all of this money now, we'll lose it."
Frank looked them in the eye and said, "So what."

Frank, seeing himself as a business partner with his customer, was guided only by the responsibility to give them the best possible advice. Anything short of that would be wrong. In the end, they saw it his way, and the customer was better for it.

Once, while giving a seminar, I was talking about the importance of preparing yourself to the point where you felt capable of, and confident enough, to say to a customer, "This is what I would do if I were you".
A young salesman told this story:

When I was first hired, Timothy really took me under his wing. I learned a lot from him, and I was lucky to have such a great guy in the next territory.
When he asked me to pick up his phone calls while he was on a weeks vacation, I was happy for the opportunity to do something for him, in return.
During that week, a customer left a message for Timothy to give him a call.
When I called the customer back, I explained that Timothy was on vacation for a week, and that I was filling in. The customer just asked that I have Timothy call him on his return. Being anxious to do something good for Timothy, I asked the customer if perhaps there wasn't something that I could do for him, then he wouldn't have to wait. The customer politely told me that he could wait, but I pushed a little harder in my efforts to do a good job for Timothy. I told the customer that if he would tell me the nature of the call, I would let Timothy know that.

I was astounded when the customer told me that he wanted Timothy's opinion on buying a product that our company didn't sell or make!
At first, I thought the customer was misinformed, but the customer was fully aware that this was not a product we were involved with. I'll never forget what he said; "I always ask Timothy's opinion before I purchase equipment, no matter what. I value his opinion."

The young salesman concluded the story by saying, "Someday I want people to think enough of me to ask for my opinions."

That is exactly what selling at the highest possible level is. Understanding your products, and the customer's circumstances. In addition, having the confidence to recommend to the customer what he should do in his business.

There are two elements that seem to be present whenever a purchase is made. (Whenever I say stuff like this, it's easy to see if you agree. Put yourself in the place of the customer, and see that if it is true about your own buying behavior.)

1. The customer believes that he has found what represents the best overall solution.

Notice that I say the best overall decision, not the best, and not the perfect decision. The best decision that I could make for my next car is a Rolls Royce. They are roomy, cool, and hold their value. However, I'm not buying a Rolls, because it's not the best overall choice for me, what with the price and all.

Considering this point reminds us that nothing that we ever buy is perfect. There are always drawbacks. However, they are drawbacks that we accept, if the product is the best overall choice for us. In cases where the product itself seems nearly perfect, it generally seems to have the drawback of being more than we intended to spend.

Keep this in mind when customers bring up a drawback. They often come up at the end of the selling process, and often just when we think the sale is imminent.

So don't get all hung up when a customer inquires about, or states something that he sees as a drawback. It's a normal part of the anguish of making decisions.

Deal with the drawback honestly, then remind the customer that your product is the best overall choice. That should be good enough. It is for me.

I was in the market for a musical instrument. I had pretty much settled on a decision to buy a Martin guitar. A friend had told me that some of the newer models were made with composite material in certain parts of the instrument. He also educated on me on the pros and cons of this.

When I was getting close to my decision, I asked the sales person, a thoroughly knowledgeable person, a question about the use of these new materials in the instrument.

Because she mistakenly thought that I saw this as negative, and a deal breaker, she immediately went from being a helpful consultant, to talking trash about the competition. It went on for a while, and she was rolling, so I just had to endure it. When she was done, I told her that I wanted the Martin.

Now she seemed confused, and said something like, "So that's all right then?" to which I responded that I was just wondering, and nothing more.

I have been guilty of the very same thing.

My boss called me for a surprise workday. One of the things on my schedule for that day was an appointment to finish up a fairly large multiple order. On our way to see the customer I told my manager that I thought it was just a matter of formalities and paperwork. They had indicated on the phone that they were very close to a decision.

I was surprised, and a little embarrassed, when very early in the meeting, someone that I had not met with before asked a technical question. He said something like, "Does this use a blankety blank, in order to blank the blank?" Knowing that this was the biggest drawback that I had to deal with on this product, I began to defend the technology, and the product.

My boss was not the kind of manager that often interjected himself into a call, unless the customer asked him something directly. He preferred to critique the call immediately upon its conclusion.

Therefore, I was surprised when he reached over and placed a hand gently on my wrist. I looked at him, and shut up for a second.
"Excuse me for just a moment," he said.
Then he looked directly at the person that had raised the drawback, and rephrased the question, by saying, "You were asking if..."
When the customer agreed, he said this to him:
"Yes, it does."
"Good," was the response.
Lesson learned.

2. The second element that has to be present for things to move toward a purchase, it that it has to be "worth it". There just has to be enough **value** in the product for us to be willing to invest in it. It is a very simple formula.

Do I think that I am going to be getting back more than I give up?

If you haven't thought this through when you get to the point where you are about to ask for the order, then I suggest that you step back a little. I can assure you that the customer has thought about it.

As a salesman, I was something of a reticent closer. Some of my reluctance came from not wanting to appear pushy, probably because of my own disdain toward pushy salesmen, and pushy people in particular.
In my mind, I had to be satisfied that if I created waaaaaaay more value for the product, relative to it's price, then the customer would see that also, and he would be delighted to move forward with a purchase.
Given my own weaknesses in closing, it was a good technique to use.

The very best salesmen, the people that I consider as business partners with their customers, always seem to take responsibility for creating and proving value for the product, and doing this in fairly specific terms.

They were prepared to discuss the impact that a product would have, both in terms of time and money.

Time and money? Aren't they the same thing in business?

I don't think that they are, at least, we tend to think of them in different ways, and some people tend to value one more than the other.
Therefore, it is important to deal with both.

No product or service really and truly makes money, unless you are selling printing equipment to the mint. (Get it?)
Particularly in manufacturing, people are looking for ways to save, or create, time. The excellent salesman can point out just how much time can be saved, and have an intelligent conversation about what to do with that time that has now been created. It is not enough just to tell people that there will be a huge timesaving. If there is no value assigned to what can be done with that time, then there is no value to be realized, and no value in making the purchase.

Curt was a small businessman. So small that he was the only employee.
He had gone into business on a shoestring a few years before I met him. To say that he was thrifty, would be saying too little.
He had some interest in our products, he had told a friend who was a happy customer that he would be interested in knowing more about the products that I sold.
Out initial conversation was only a few minutes old when he asked the price. He choked on it, and I was surprised when he said he thought it was less than half of that.
The conversation slowed down considerably from there, and I was certain that it wasn't going anywhere anyway.
Curt began bemoaning his decision to go into business in the first place. He was explaining to me that he was not accomplishing what he wanted to.
He continued by saying that he had always worked long hours, and had made the decision to go out on his own, so that he could spend more time with his sons. He had always dreamed that he would be their soccer coach, but since going into business for

85

himself, he barely had time to make it to see the games, let alone making the additional time investment necessary for coaching. We began to discuss the possibility that if he invested in new technology, perhaps that would create some time for him. This intrigued Curt, and he commented that he had to work such long hours, just to meet customer demands for delivery.

We began to study specific examples. We began to arrive at time savings that were substantial, but not enough to create the time necessary. Curt concluded that with more automation, his own involvement in making stuff was far less important.

After a fairly grueling couple of hours going over the exact amount of time that a purchase would create, Curt decided that one product would just not do it for him, so he bought two. And, he coached his boys at soccer.

Certainly, this is an extreme and an unusual example. That's the main reason that I have included it here, and probably why I remember it.

We need to help our customers think through what the impact of an investment is in this way. How much time will it save or create for me, and how can I put that time to good use?

Can the time savings be used to reduce overtime, and therefore reduce costs? Can employees take on other tasks? Can the workforce be reduced?

They say that time is money. That's true, but only if the time is put to good use.

Money? How much money?

Just as in time savings, top sales professionals help prospects and customers figure out exactly how much money can be saved (made) on an investment. They see it as a necessary part of the job, and a responsibility that goes with encouraging someone to invest. Reduced down, it's like saying, "If you give me this, I'll help you get that". But how does this money actually get made?

Well, the answer lies in the response that you will often hear a customer make. They have to speak to accounting. Or, they have to complete paperwork that indicates the precise return on investment.

Why would you do otherwise?

The reason for being in business is to make profit, not to employ people. Profit. And if you are asking someone to invest in your products or services, then you should damn well be prepared to discuss the amount of profit that you will be helping them to generate.

Many, many salesmen ignore this part of their job completely. Top salesmen never do. Top salesmen have learned what is necessary for them to know about accounting, and cost accounting.

I am not suggesting that salesmen become accountants. Accounting is a science all of it's own. What I am suggesting, however, is that salesmen act like *businessmen.*

Do you really think that customers believe salesmen that say things like "You will make tons of money with this," or "You'll make so much money you won't know what to do with it!" Or, "This will be great for your bottom line."

If you want to get to the top in the world of sales, you will need to study the basics of accounting, and the principles of cost accounting that are used by your customers.

Even if you are selling a commodity product, businessmen know that there is a difference between the price, and the cost. If you sell bearings that are more expensive than someone else's, the belief is that the customer will get something more from that bearing. What is the "more" that they will get, and what are the cost savings associated with it?

If the price of your bearing is one dollar more than the competition, but lasts longer, what are the cost savings? How does this impact the customer positively, in accounting terms?

If you are selling some sort of automation, the equipment, or software has a price. This price is to be used to calculate the effectiveness of the product.

Businessmen understand that the price will not be absorbed all at once like a sunk cost, or the money that they spend on vacation.

The price is put in its appropriate place. The amount of time that the product is amortized is decided on, relative to tax code. The cost of the equipment is then related to time, just like the wages and costs of employees are related to time. How much does the equipment cost per hour to run?

You need to understand the costs of people. It is not just their wages, but also, all of the other contributions that the employer must make on their behalf, plus their contribution to paying for all of the other costs that the business has, such as power, heat, light and indirect employees. Overhead.

If the money needs to be borrowed, then it has a cost. That needs to be considered, and added to the mix. However, if you can borrow a dime to make a dollar, then it's generally thought to be a good investment. Unless, that is, the interest on the dime is ninety cents.

It all comes down to this:

At the time when you are suggesting to the customer that he should purchase the product or system that you have enlightened him on, you are really saying:

If you give me this, you will get that.

This doesn't have to be presented down to the nickel. As I said, you are a salesman, not an accountant. However, you need to be able to say something like:

Here is what I came up with. You have told me that your costs are X.
If you invest this many dollars, we can see that it will reduce the time by this much.
Using the facts that you have given me for the hourly burden rate of your employees (often rounded off as 1.5 times the average wage) we can see that this investment will cost you an additional number of dollars, or cents, per hour.
And, it will save you this number of minutes per part.
Since we know that a minute costs you this much in labor, then you can see that an investment of X, will reduce your costs by Y.

If you can't follow that, I suggest that you invest some time to understand how cost accountants and project managers think, when they are recommending if your product or system should be purchased. I'll give one more example, for the uninitiated. Then, I'll make my conclusion.

A person runs a machine, making widgets (I wish there was another word like widget)
        The operator is paid $16.00 per hour.
Fully loaded, his cost to his employer adds another $4, for benefits, etc.
His contribution to overhead adds another $5 per hour.
Therefore, he has a total *cost* of $25 per hour.
These are generally accepted approximate numbers. If customers can tell you their own hourly burden rate, plus average wage, use them.
Anyway, the person costs $25 per hour, or 42 cents per minute.
Every ten minutes, he completes a part. 10 minutes, at 42 cents per minute means that the labor cost is $4.20 each part.

The machine that he currently makes the widgetry on, has a **price** of $21,000.00
We need to get this cost into the same "per hour" idea as the labor.
Their company says that they can fully amortize equipment over seven years.
So, the machine **costs** $3000 per year.
They use the machine on a one-shift basis, most of the time.
They figure that it runs 1500 of the 2000 hours that are available every year, for one shift.
So, if you divide the $3000 by the 1500 hours, the machine **costs** $2 per hour to run, or about 3-1/2 cents per minute.
So, 10 minutes costs .35 (machine cost)
Add that to the labor ($4.20), and the **cost** of the part is $4.55 ea.

You have proposed that they buy your equipment, to reduce the running time. Their quandary is this. Is it worth it?

Lets see.

The **price** of the new machine is $28,000.00 (a big increase, a big investment.)
Using the same formula as above, the **cost** of the machine is:
28,000 divided by 7=4000
4000 divided by 1500= $2.67 per hour, or about 4-1/2 cents per minute.
Therefore, we have raised the cost by a known amount per minute.

Tests have proven that the cycle time for the new machine goes from 10 minutes apiece, to 7.
So, 7 minutes of labor (@ 42 cents per minute) equals $2.94.
That is the new labor cost for each part.
The new machine, with its higher cost of 4.5 cents per minute is now included.
7 minutes, at 4.5 cents, means that the machine cost is now $.32

Add the $2.94 to the .32, and the **cost** for the part is now $3.26.
This includes both the higher cost of the machine, and the decreased time to manufacture.

Old **Cost**= $4.55/ ea.
New **Cost**=$3.26/ ea.

Is it worth it? That's up to the customer. By applying a little science to it (unknown to many of us salesmen), we can say something like:

With your current set-up, you make widgets at the rate of ten per hour, for 1500 hours in a year.
That's 15000 parts per year.
*With your current **cost** of $4.55 per part, that totals an annual cost of $68,250.00*

If you make the investment that I am suggesting, your annual costs are $48,900.00

That is a cost reduction, in the first year alone, of $19,350. The machine is paid for in less than two years.
Sounds like a good investment to me. What do you think?

On the other hand, of course, you can stick with some of the other things I have heard salesman say, truly motivating comments like:

- *You'll make so much money; you won't know what to do with it.*
  - *Faster has got to be better, right?*
  - *You'll get your money back in no time.*
  - *It's good bang for the buck.*

The discovery that I hope you are making, is this:

The truly successful sales people, the ones that take a sincere interest in partnering with their customers, behave as though they are solving their own problems, and their own money that they are spending. They go through each of the following steps:

1. They understand what the customer wants to achieve, and why.
2. Once they understand the problem, if (and only if), they have a solution; they present it, thoroughly.
3. They discuss the actual benefit that the customer should get for their investment.
4. They recommend the solution that they have suggested, because it meets all the criteria from number 1.
5. They encourage them, if necessary.

If you miss any one of the steps, it all collapses like a house of cards.

If you make all of the steps, you provided true help to the customer, you have differentiated yourself from all of the bonehead sales people out there, and you have behaved like a businessman.

Moreover, you deserved to be rewarded for it.

As Zig Ziglar says "If you help enough other people get what they want, some day you'll be able to get everything that you want."

Chapter 9

Are You Improving?

Or,

Are you awesome enough already?

Self Improvement

This may be the shortest chapter in this book. It may also be the most important.

A man went to his annual review feeling confident. He had finished a fairly good year and had exceeded all of the minimum goals that had been established for him. He was tops in a few product categories.

His manager began the review with this question. "What are you planning to improve on in the next year?" Quite honestly, he hadn't given that topic very much thought, so he went with a weak reply. "Sell more?" he asked, hoping that it would be a satisfactory answer.
"Sell more what?" the manager asked.
He had no genuine reply, so he just sat there. The manager went on to ask if self-improvement was an area that he thought that he was diligent enough about. Since he had not considered it much as he planned for this review, he had to concede that it was not an important topic for him.
"You had a good year," he was told. You can be proud of what you have accomplished. But unless that's good enough for you, you need to be serious about strengthening your weakest areas.

Good advice is pretty hard to argue with, so he didn't. The boss went on to carve up his job functions and responsibilities, until they agreed on the areas that needed the most improvement. The manager didn't bash the salesman with the discovery of his weaknesses, he simply identified them, and they agreed on them.
He then set the salesman on the task of reflecting on his weaker areas, and what he might do to improve. The discussion was then tabled for two weeks.
The salesman was prepared when they met again, and he presented his written plan for improvement, including milestones. The boss helped him throughout the year, and they went over things quarterly. It might have been the single most important lesson of the salesman's career.
The manager never really lectured the salesman. It was his style to inspire people to do better, and he knew that people always made their own best ideas work the best.

It is my hope that you will be able to identify a few weaknesses in my list of nine, and create a plan for improvement. If your greatest challenge is not on my list, but you are still encouraged to beef up your weaker areas, then we still have accomplished something together.

However, once you arrive at your decision, you need a plan.

Take any area of your job, and give serious thought to your weakest areas. Sometimes these areas are easy to define, but not always. For instance, if you know that you are a disorganized slob, and you are always searching for missing data about customers, wondering when your appointments are, and searching for your keys, it's fairly easy to say that you need to get organized. However, changing a habit is not that easy.

Here are some steps that I suggest to help in changing a habit:

1. Shine a light on it. Just becoming aware of a self-imposed obstacle should help to improve.
2. Think it through, where are the obstacles? Make a list of do's and don'ts.
3. Create Milestones. Come up with a regularly scheduled method to see if you are staying on track.
4. Ask someone successful. Find someone that does what you do, but they do it better. Ask them for help and advice. Find out their methods, their systems, and their mind set, and then copy what they do.
5. Go outside the circle. Find stuff to read on the topic, and get fresh ideas.
6. Set Goals! How else will you know how you're doing?

One of the problems with self-improvement is that it can be hard to analyze your activities fairly. The best thing is to examine the results, more than the process.

Ed was looking for some help in selling. He was an overly confident guy, in my view, so I knew that asking for help wasn't that easy. He was busy blaming things like stupid customers, the economy, prices, and a lousy territory for his low level of success.

It was pretty clear to me that he was making at least one fundamental mistake after just two sales calls, but I held my critique for the end of the workday.

When he asked me what I thought, I told him that it seemed to me that he had only a superficial understanding of his customers. I began to explain, but he cut me off in order to tell me about his good probing skills. I began to ask him about the definition of probing, when he began to recite a few examples of his excellent questions.

*I endeavored to ask him if he knew **all** about his customer's circumstances, that is, specifically what and why a customer needs; but I didn't get to. He had moved onto telling me about a recent great sales call he had made.*

Finally, I asked him if he wanted my help or not. He looked bewildered, and a little angry. He said that he certainly did want my help.

Then I pointed out that he had interrupted me three times in one short conversation. When I pointed out where and when, he agreed sheepishly. I was then able to point out, and illustrate that he had done this to his customers all day.

I encouraged him to be just as enthusiastic in his belief in his products, but to slow down in telling them that he had the perfect solution to a problem that he was assuming that they had.

Furthermore, I added, wanting to make the most important observation that I had made, I said, "When you ask someone a question, you should let them answer, completely. You should keep asking questions until you understand completely. Just as importantly, it is rude to continually interrupt people, so that you can talk."

Ed agreed, saying that his wife told him that he did that all the time.

Ed wasn't aware that he was such a poor listener, but to his credit, he used the criticism as inspiration to improve. He went back to some earlier training that he had received, regarding listening, and asking probing questions. He stayed in touch with me a few more times, just to be sure that he was making progress, which he was.

Ed needed help on discovering his self-imposed obstacles, which brings me to my next point.

7. Find a Coach. Find someone that you trust, that will listen to you as you talk about the difficult situations that you face. It

might be your manager, but it might also be another salesperson, or someone outside of your organization that you respect. Don't look so much for the Coach to give you solutions. A good coach can offer solid critique on the obstacles that you are creating for yourself. Removing them is up to you. Who better?

A final word on self-improvement.

It has been an observation of mine that some people are obviously continually working on improving. It is obvious in their conversations, just as it is in the way that they seem to view their place in the world.

The real observation is that the most successful people are always looking for ways to improve. Now maybe that should be obvious, but wouldn't you expect that the people who clearly demonstrate their weakness in a particular area to be about the work of getting better? It should be, but it ain't.

There are tons of stories from the world of sports about the best athlete on the team being the hardest working. Why is this so? My sense is that is because it is their **habit** to improve. They have integrated critical observation, practice, and improvement into the way that they think.

My Dad, a particularly hardworking man, always said to me "It is amazing what you can accomplish in just one hour." I have learned that to be true, and have attempted to pass it along to my own children.

Tasks that I know that I have procrastinated on, when I finally tackle them, seldom take as long as I feared they would. I believe that it is the similar with the work that we need to do when we want to improve. It can seem that the work will be so overwhelming that we just don't get started.

I admire a well-kept lawn. I often drive by one lawn that seemed to have that golf course quality. It was so nice that you couldn't help but notice it on the way by. I certainly did. On one occasion, as I passed this home, I noticed a man outside. I pulled into the drive, and asked him for a minute of his time.

"How is that your lawn is so perfect?" I asked, expecting the answer to be a type of sod, or fertilizer, or maybe an expensive lawn service.
The man smiled and said, "That's my Pop's department, let me get him."
Pop seemed to be a particularly spry gentleman of about 80.
"You like my lawn?" he asked. I told him that I always admired it on my way by. "What's your secret?" I asked him.
"Oh, that's easy," he said smiling. "I work on it for a half an hour every day."

I believe that's the way it is with self-improvement. In my own experience, I have learned that it is not about making some Herculean effort that dies out in a few weeks, and it's not like cramming for a test in college.

It's about the habit. Having the mindset of wanting to improve, continually.

If you don't have an hour, or even a half-hour a day to work on improving, well then…

Chapter 10

Are You a Good Employee?

Chances are, if you are a great salesman, you are not a great employee. That's not a completely bad thing. However, to be a great salesman, you have to least be a good employee.

Many salesmen are mavericks. That is partly what draws them to the world of sales. They treasure their independence, and they don't like being told what to do every second of every day. They want to make their own schedules, and use their own approach to things. Lots of salesmen want to skip all of the paperwork that isn't directly associated to them getting paid, (a genuine piss-off for managers and office folks.)

As sales people, we can sometimes take a peculiarly insular view of our importance. Consider this absolutely astounding story.

Davis was a pretty fair salesman, and a champion of one particular product. The product that he favored was a lower end product, so he needed to sell lots of them to make much money. He didn't quite see it that way.
With great bravado, he wrote a letter to the president of the company, to explain why his commission on this product should be much higher.
He made a long list of all of the costs of the product that he could think of. He listed the commission, shipping, guessed at some marketing and advertising costs. He figured in the expenses of the salesman. After making this "comprehensive" list, he subtracted the costs from the selling price, using the enormous margin as his tool to argue for a higher commission. He reasoned that if the company was going to make a bundle, so should he.
He received a terse note back from the president.
The president pointed out that in all of his calculations, he left out one thing. He failed to list the cost of the product.

We really have to keep in mind that although we are the people that the customers come to know and depend on, we are only one of the pieces that makes a company successful.
Long before we go to work, someone had to envision the product. It had to be designed, tested, and debugged. It had to go through cost engineering, so that a good product could be made as cheaply as possible.
Marketing had to create awareness in a particular market segment.

Accounting and manufacturing had to work with everyone else to arrive at a fair price.

Materials had to be bought, equipment purchased or designed, and somebody had to manufacture the products that you sell.

Product literature and advertising had to be created.

And more…and more…

My guess is that if a company went to all that fuss and bother, they would figure out some way to get the product to market, if you didn't do it for them.

As a salesman, I had a few opportunities to sell a product that was so advanced, and powerful, that I had a huge advantage over all of the competitors. It was a product that customers could see immediately as being a great value. I did nothing to earn this, other than working for the right company. I am encouraging you to be sensible about that, perhaps even a little grateful.

It is important to take a somewhat egalitarian view of your job, and the sales that you make.

For any deal or sale to be *good* it needs to be equally good for you, the customer, and your employer. Anything else is a bad deal. Be aware of this when looking for huge price concessions from your employer. Every dollar taken off of the price of a product is going to have be subtracted from somewhere, and if you don't want it to be taken from your commission, it will have to come from some place else.

Often, the softer costs are affected first, like advertising, and that is bad for everyone in the company. Keep in mind, also, that companies like to use the margin from successful products, to develop new ones. You like new products, right?

How to be a lousy employee.

1. Sell only the products that you like, or think will give you the best return on your investment of time.
2. Be habitually late with paperwork and reports, even with the knowledge that you are creating a problem for someone else. Always have a cute story when you do this.

100

3. Seize those opportunities that salesmen have to do things when no one is watching. Do your shopping and play golf during working hours. Always be the one that drives the kids places, because, after all, your spouse has to be at work.
4. Look out for number one, exclusively. After all, your pay is based partially on your own performance.
5. Keep all of your thoughts to yourself, except for when you want to whine. Be sure to complain directly to your customers about the things you don't like about your employer.
6. Constantly remind everyone of any possible competitive disadvantage, and why that is the reason that you lose orders.

How to be a good employee.

1. Embrace the entire product line, being certain that customers understand all that you can do for them. Make the appropriate efforts so that your employer can be active in all of the market segments that are deemed to be important.
2. Follow the rules of reporting as they are set out for you. If you can be a day late with paperwork, you can be a day early.
3. Understand that all that your employer owes you is the opportunity to make a good living. What you owe in return is an honest days work, and maybe a little extra.
4. Be a team player. Meet any reasonable requests from your manager, and keep in mind that you have a responsibility to help out the new salesmen. Become the person that they go to for advice.
5. When you have a valid complaint, do so thoughtfully, and always complain "up" in the organization, where something can actually be done about the situation.
6. Help to improve your products, by translating the needs of customers to your employer.

But what if my boss is a moron?

I hate to break the news to you, but this is going to happen. In fact, if it only happens once, you are leading a charmed life.

It seems that many times, a great, or at least a good salesman, is promoted into management, because of his success in selling.
I always thought it was better to have a boss that could do what I do. Sales managers that have beat the streets always seemed to have empathy for what it's like out there, and their advice is generally more practical than theoretical.

And then there are times when they are bullies, or the kind of boss that insists that you do things exactly in the way that they did them.

Well, poor you.

Even the worst boss has something to offer. Try to look for the positive. It is also helpful to recognize that someone higher up the chain thought enough of this person to promote them. It is only fair that you give them a chance.
If they are really that awful, have enough confidence in the system that supports them to recognize the shortcomings, and reevaluate their decision. Perhaps they will receive some training, or some advice. And perhaps they will be replaced.

It has been my experience that the truly poor sales managers often figure it out for themselves, and return to the ranks. It's either that, or they are replaced. You have a responsibility to wait it out sometimes. Try to remain a gentleman.

Also, try to keep your expectations in line. We're all just folks after all, and like a seasoned salesman said to me once when I became his manager. "I guess I better get to work. It takes a while to break in a new boss."

I had hired a salesman that had been let go by a competitor, when the economy forced them to shrink the sales force.
I never really got along very well with him, although I did try. I did hear lots of stories about the awesome boss that he had at his last place of employment.

Well, he quit. On his exit interview, he let me know how little he thought of me as a boss, and I encouraged him to provide some examples to illustrate my many shortcomings.

He reminded me that the economy was bad when he came to us, and that was why he had lost his old job. That was true, the economy had been really bad.

"In all those times," he said, "when things were so rough out there, you never once said to me, 'lets skip work today, and go out and play golf. I know how hard you have been trying."

I was more than a little surprised. It had never occurred to me that the panacea for not selling was a day on the golf course. Perhaps that's the way it was at the old place, but it sure wasn't like that for me.
Still, I got his point. He wanted some recognition for his efforts, and I probably hadn't provided enough, or any.
The truth is, that's just not my way.

Nevertheless, somewhere in there, there were some missed expectations. I'll leave it to you to figure out whom to blame.

The point of the story is that we shouldn't put unrealistic, and unspoken expectations on each other.
It tends to complicate a relationship that is supposed to be mutually beneficial.

If you find that you become saddled with a boss that is dishonest, that is their problem. If, however, you are expected to be dishonest, that's different.

If you find that you have a boss that is a prick, that's his problem. If, however, you are being treated in a way that is *personally* harmful to you, (you know, insulting, condescending) that's different.

If either of those conditions exists, to the point where it affects your sleep, or your relationships at home, then you should quit.

Just be sure that you have at least considered talking with others in the organization, and you really can't endure it.

By all means, don't make an emotional decision to quit; you may regret it. Like all major decisions, if it's a good idea today, it will still be a good idea tomorrow.

Chapter 11

Motion and Action

Motion and Action

Some smart person (it might have been Ben Franklin, but I don't feel like looking it up, and besides, it doesn't matter who said it) said:

"Don't confuse motion with action."

Or, as I like to think of it, "You can work your butt off trying to cut down a tree with a penknife, but you ain't getting very far any time soon."

I have found that this applies to selling in a unique way. So often, we do something (Action) and believe that the customer has moved closer to making a purchase. (Motion)

Haven't we all had experiences like this? We do something, or tell something to a customer, believe that a sale is imminent, and then learn on our next contact with the customer that he hasn't really given the matter any more thought?

At sales seminars, I often ask the participants to shout out what their biggest obstacles and challenges are. In short, I ask, "What's hard about selling?"
One of the topics that always makes the list is "stuck" customers.
We do some work, make (or believe we make) some progress, and then we just feel "stuck." Stuck, because we don't have a clue what to do next.
Sales people often recognize that since they don't really know what to do, they sort of begin to pester the customer, hoping that something has changed. Since it hasn't, the contact that they make is sometimes negative, and usually pointless.

At the seminars, I present an idea that I use to understand a stalled selling process. It is intended to help the salesman figure out where the customer is in the selling process, so he can figure out what the next logical work is. The hope is that you can use it to "unstick" customers, but what is more important, is how to prevent it from happening in the first place. It's not a perfect system, but it can be helpful.

Here are the most important points to remember:

1. It is the job of the salesman to take responsibility for driving the process.
2. In any selling job, regardless of the product or service, there are certain things that you can do. Things that have to be done. Just as with any job that needs to be done, you can come up with a list of tasks.
3. It's not what you do, (action) that matters. What matters is what the customer accepts. (Motion)
4. A method is needed to pinpoint what process customers go through on their way to buying.
5. Once the buying process is identified, you need to be clear on what the customer has accepted.
6. Know what to do, or have a few ideas, on what you might do, at each stage of acceptance.

Looking first at the stuff that we can do, here is a list of salesman activities. If it is incomplete for you, just stick in the work that you can do for customers, as it applies.

1. Identify a customer as a prospect or suspect. (Research)
2. Confirm the potential for your business. Is there a reason for you to be calling on this customer?
3. Identify the contacts. All of them. Certainly, you want to identify the best person for you to be working with initially, but who are all of the people that can say no to buying your products? This would include the folks who would use your products, but it also includes floor management, engineering, purchasing, senior management, and the money folks. Getting to know them, or at least who they are early in the process might just be helpful later on.
4. Working with your primary contact, learn where the roadblocks are. That is, what is their problem? What are their circumstances? How *well* are their current products or systems working for them? What is it that they want to fix, solve, alleviate, or improve on?
5. Since your new contact may not be too forthcoming about telling you all about their problems, (how freely do you share information with people that you don't know well?), ask for an opportunity to give them a very global introduction to your company, products, and your own background.

6. Introduce product families, or specific products, that help with what the customer is trying to accomplish.
7. Offer every means necessary, to fully explain or illustrate the product. This might include brochures, testimonials, references, videos, presentations, and product demonstrations. All of this work is about teaching the customer about the product, and similar applications where it has worked.
8. Prove it. If the customer learns, but isn't satisfied, what will make him a believer? Does he need to use it? Speak to others? Get third party information? Learn where the skepticism is, and deal with it directly.
9. Prove the impact. You just gotta do the work regarding cost. How much time will it save? How much will it lower cost? How much better will things be after they own it?
10. Recommend it. Say what you would do, and why. Summarize all that has been accomplished, and be prepared to go over *everything.*
11. Ask for the order.

That section was about the things that **you** do. It includes all of the steps that I can think of that may need to be covered.

If you have gone all the way through that process, and the customer has declined, that's O.K.
Either you will get a "not now," to which you will apply your refined questioning skills, to find out, "when." Sometimes we just have to wait for something to occur on their end, or to follow the budget process.

However, if you are somewhere else in the process, you might be finding that your prospect is unwilling or disinterested in going further. Why? Because he hasn't accepted what you think he has accepted.

The next section takes a look at the buying process from the customer point of view.

As always, check this out against your own process when you are a customer, to see if the theories hold up.

It is my contention that folks go through a buying process with a reasonable level of predictability. Not that *people* are predictable, but that there is a kind of flow chart that we follow, from the time that we first learn about something, until the moment that we buy it.

Here are the steps.

1. I don't really know what it is.
2. I understand what it is, and how it works.
3. I understand the value of this product, for me. That is, I think that it is "worth it."
4. I know how to buy it today, given my current financial situation.
5. I want it, and I want it now.

I don't really know what it is.

Perhaps this is a little too fundamental to point out, but it occurs to me that many of the things that we buy, we start off being curious about. Maybe this isn't true of a dishwasher, or a car, but it might be if it's an MP3 player, or some other technology product. In any case, sometime we just don't understand something, either partially or fully, and that is our starting point. For example, I think I know what a time-share is, but I don't really know very much about how they work.

I understand what it is, and how it works.

This is the first stage that we complete for products that we buy. Again, it's not that we are completely ignorant on the topic, but there is a lot that we have to learn. This would include the actual, "how does it work," portion, as well as "what comes with it." This is where we learn about what is included, and what is optional. At this stage, we want to know about features, models, sizes, etc.

I understand the value of this product, for me. That is, I think that it is "worth it."

As the process continues, for the products that we ultimately purchase, once we know "how it works," and all of the details that surround that, we begin earnestly wrestling with the price of it. If the price seems, "worth it," to us, then somewhere between this step, and the previous step, **desire** is created. We begin to think that this is something that we want.

Therefore, as customers, we are thinking about **value**. The bright salesman will assist here, helping the customer to figure out the one and only thing about the value that matters. At this stage, we are asking ourselves, "Is it worth it, **to me?**"

If we go through step one, and learn all about a camera that seems to have all of the things we need, and then learn that the price tag is $5000.00, it may just not be worth it to us. If it is $500.00, it starts to seem about right, but we are wrestling with it. If it goes on sale for $300.00, we snatch it up, because the value is absolutely clear to us.

The salesman may have to do as much work in this section as in the first section, where we are describing product features, and talking about goodies. Don't be the kind of salesman, like Will, that doesn't think that this section is important.

Will complained long, loud, and often, about the price of the products he was selling. He was really hung up on the fact that he did a marvelous job talking about his product, but more times than not, they didn't buy once they heard the price.

Therefore, he came to the conclusion that the price was too high, and there was nothing that he could do about it. So, he gave up on those customers.

When he got the chance to complain, at a National Sales Meeting, he was vocal, and critical to everyone in management, for putting the salesman in an untenable position.

I think that Will was very brave for telling me this story, as he looks so foolish in it, but he recognized that he had learned something important.

The speaker asked if everyone agreed with Will, and some did. About a third, he guessed. The speaker than asked Will, and the others that agreed with him, if they thought it was worth the price. Will, and most of the others clearly believed that it was not, as evidenced by the response of customers. He then asked the other two thirds if they thought it was worth the price, and they believed it was. The speaker then said to Will, "If you don't think it's worth it, neither will your customers."

*Then, it got even juicier. The speaker asked "If I knocked 10 percent off the price, would it be worth it then?" Will said no. The speaker got a few laughs from the audience, reminding Will that this was how much was added on for his commission. Then he asked if the price was reduced by 30 percent, if it would be worth it. Will heartily agreed that that would do it; it would be a "no brainer." The speaker then explained that the full value of a product is rarely self-imminent. The job of the salesman, and his worth to the organization, was in his ability to help people **understand the value**. Then, to make his point, he said, "Look Will, if we lowered the price by 50 Percent, we wouldn't need a sales force at all.*

I know how to buy it today, given my current financial situation.

Once we understand both "What it is and how it works," along with "It is worth it, to me," Desire for the product has been created. We want it, and we want it right now. That explains why customers that have been unwilling to buy a product for a very long time, need it tomorrow when they finally decide. Something has changed about their circumstance that has brought them to a place in which they understand the value.

Consider your own buying habits here. If you want something (desire), and you have the cash, you pay for it. If not, then you whip out a credit card, get a loan, or a mortgage, or ask your parents for the money.
Speaking as a parent, I see this as a bad idea.

Sometimes we are even willing to sell something that we own, to get what we want, now.

Once people truly understand the value of something, and therefore desire it, they want it. Now.

The work for the sales person is to help them to achieve this, given their current financial situation. If they can't, or won't, pay for it now in full, then you need to educate them on the payment strategies that are available to them. You may have some programs available from your own company, but if not, you need to find the leasing and lending institutions that might help them. Don't assume anything about this. You will most likely be wrong.

As a young salesman, I had forecast a quite sizeable order for the current month. The customer had made it clear that he wanted to buy, and asked for some help on suggesting a leasing company, which I did. The customer said clearly that he wanted it, but he would have to lease it.
I learned that they had not qualified for the lease, so I knew that there was no sale.
When my boss asked me about this sale that I had forecast, and then removed, I explained the situation to him.
He said to me, "How will they pay for it then?" I reexplained that it was clear from the beginning. No lease=No deal.
The bossman encouraged me to visit the customer, and say these words, "Since the lease idea didn't work out, how do you plan to pay for it?"

I had no confidence that this was worthwhile, but partly out of my respect for the bossman, and partly out of the delicious idea of being right, I did as I was told.

The customer and I chatted for a moment, including the acknowledgment that the lease wasn't approved. I said, "Since the lease idea didn't work out, how do you want to pay for it?"
He said, "I guess I'll have to use some funds that I didn't really want to touch."

Once people desire something, they will move heaven and earth to get it.
The wise sales person will help them to find the best way for them, given their current financial situation.

I want it, and I want it now.

I am fairly certain that once a customer pronounces these words, you know what to do.

Okay, so that's all good in theory, but…

It stops being a theory if it works. Here is the way that I put it to use.

I consider the "stuck" customer carefully. I do that, because I really don't have a clue why he is unwilling to move forward, when I am so sure that he has a strong application.

The first question that I ask myself is this. I am a working with the right person? I mean, is this the person that can decide, or influence the decision with others? Fairly fundamental I know, but worthy of consideration when you are stuck. Keep in mind that sometimes people act like they have a bit more authority then they actually do. You just might be dealing with someone that can't do anything about purchasing, or they might be unwilling to suggest any idea that might rock the boat, and make them look bad.

The people that are unable to make a final decision regarding a purchase, usually offer clues as to whom they really are. By this, I mean how they view themselves, as well as how others see them, in the hierarchy of their organization.

Listen to, or recall what they say very carefully. There are two types.

1. **A bridge.** This is the type that understands the application, but is not in a position to make a buying decision. Still, he sees himself as an important link, and understands his role. Since these folks see themselves as a part of something, they refer to their co-workers, and management as "we." They might say things like:
    -   We don't buy equipment without board approval.
    -   We are always open to new ideas.
    -   We are not in a position to buy now; budgets have been cut.

112

- We buy everything at the end of our fiscal year.

I characterize these people by their behavior, as a "bridge," They will become a bridge between you and the folks that decide. Asking them for help in moving up to the right people is generally rewarded.

2. **A Wall.** This type is far more irritating, and not often helpful, because they see themselves as being outside the circle of influence. They usually will not do anything useful in terms of helping you get up the ladder, because they see it as either pointless, or they fear (correctly) that they won't be taken seriously by the higher-ups. Since they don't see themselves as part of a larger group, they say things like:

   - They don't have any idea what we need around here.
   - They never get me anything.
   - These people don't know what they're doing.

I characterize these people as a "wall," because, although they may understand and support the use of your stuff, but they won't get involved in pushing it further. In fact, if you ask them to tell you whom you should speak with regarding this great application, you will hear something like, "They wouldn't know a good idea if they fell over it."

Therefore, you have to go over the wall, or around the wall. Going over their head may irritate them, but it doesn't matter. Chances are that management thinks as little of him, as he does of them. This is quite different from dealing with the "bridge" type of person. If you go over them, or around them, you run the risk of irritating them, because they are inclined to help.

Now then, having reviewed the situation, and feeling certain that you are talking with all of the right people, you begin by looking at things from the customer's point of view. Ask yourself these questions:
1. Do they really understand the product well enough?
2. Do they really see the value in it?

3. Do they have the money? Do they know about all of their choices in paying for this?

If you can clearly see what steps they have accepted, then go back and start off on the next one. Even when you think that you covered it all before, it doesn't matter what you have said. It matters what they have accepted.

If you're not sure, you are far better off to go back a step, than to skip one.

Formulate your opening by saying something like:

The reason I am here is to discuss more fully what this product will really do for you, in terms of saving time. I am prepared to talk about specific examples. Would that be helpful?

After that, you have got to listen, because their response should clearly tell you where they are in the process. They might say:

1. I think we can see what it will do for us, but I'm not sure if it makes enough difference for the money.
He is telling you that it's not worth it to him, so working on the value part would be correct.
2. I am not sure if it is going to do all of the things that we need it to do.
He is telling you that he doesn't fully understand all of the physical characteristics and choices regarding your product. Go back to the previous step.
3. I can see how it's a good investment for us. We just have to figure out where the money is coming from.
He is telling you that he most likely understands the value, but doesn't know all of his finance choices.

4. Now that you understand where the customer *really* is in the process, get to work by applying all of those wonderful things that you can do for him, from the first section about salesman activities that will drive the process. Apply what fits. For example, if he said "I think we can see what it will do for us, but I'm not sure if it makes enough difference for the money," then it might be appropriate to consider Number 9 from above.

Prove the impact. You just gotta do the work regarding

*cost. How much time will it save? How much will it lower
cost? How much better will things be after they own it?*

Consider things like a cost justification, or actually doing a
comparative and factual study about the difference between his
methods, and yours.
Then be sure to roll up the difference, so that you both can see
the real savings in time, and the true potential for lowering cost.

Some sales people found that the more fully they adopt this
thinking into their everyday sales work, the fewer customers that
are likely to get stuck.
As the customer demonstrates acceptance at each level, it is
easier to create a plan to move forward.

Most importantly, you are using the appropriate tools to satisfy
each level of customer acceptance, before randomly moving into
another area.

On the other hand, of course, you can wing it.

Chapter 12

Matters of Style

Matters of Style

Often, at sales training seminars, people will reference something that I have said, and ask, "I like to do it this way, is that all right?"

My frequent response is that I just don't argue with matters of style.

I simply don't see the point in long arguments, just to insist that my way is better. I don't say this about bad habits, or following the fundamentals of selling. I am not saying that it is okay to disregard the importance of good listening skills, or the need for organization. What I am saying is that you need to apply good habits, and use your own beliefs and personality to do so.

I was talking about the need to get down to business early in the sales call, to let the customer know that you are not interested in a lot of small talk, or wasting time. I believe that this is critical as we begin to get to know a new prospect, so that they don't think that you only stopped by to "visit with them."

The people that I was speaking to were mostly from the southern states, and they go about things differently than in the Northeastern corridor, or the Midwest, or the West Coast. At least that's what they told me.
One seasoned salesman took great umbrage at what I was saying, and let me know about it. He explained that he knew his customers, and their families, and their likes and dislikes. He continued that he often would spend half an hour discussing fishing with them. He lectured me about the importance of building rapport.

I responded that I thought rapport was better established while working on a problem that the customer had. I also said that I never would spend half an hour talking about fishing, or football, or any other non-business matter. I continued that I saw it as a waste of his time, as well as mine.
I watched him become angry as I spoke, and I had to stop him from interrupting me several times, so that I could make my whole point.
I continued by saying that if you think that is important, and your customers don't object, then, by all means, do what feels comfortable for you.
"But which one is right?" he demanded.

I believe that there is no "right way," regarding matters of style, and I said so.
However, I insisted that good salesmanship demands that you let the customer know, quite clearly, when it is time to get down to business. This lets them know that you are a serious businessman that came to his office for a business purpose.

I answered in this way. " Whether you build rapport for three minutes or 30 is up to you. I just don't argue with matters of style."

In point of fact, I think that it is important that you develop your own unique style, the one that genuinely reflects your true personality. You will be displaying the very best version of yourself, by having the confidence to be whoever you are. Certainly you can do that, while you develop the habits that lead to success.

Some comments about style.

Questions often come up about how to dress. I am amazed that there can be so many pages in so many sales books dedicated to this one issue. I am not convinced that you can actually "dress for success," unless you are in a singles bar. Not that dress is unimportant; I am just suggesting that it isn't the thing that assures that you close a sale. I do concede, however, that you can turn people off if you show up looking like pimp daddy, or Jethro Bodine in the world of business. Here are my thoughts:

1. Your dress should be appropriate. It is not hard to figure out what that means for the business that you are in.
2. You need to be neat. Like it or not, we associate slovenliness with laziness. If you wear cotton shirts and a necktie, don't go out looking like you ironed your shirt with a rock.
3. Try not to draw immediate attention to yourself with jewelry, cologne, piercings, tattoos, rainbow hair, Mohawks, tee shirts with stupid slogans on them, or shirts intended for a Jimmy Buffet concert. It doesn't matter so much if your hair is long or short, if it is neat. Moreover, keep within your own style.

My friend Charlie wears suits that cost more than some of my cars. I am not saying that he is "flashy," just that he is dressed far better than nearly everyone he meets with. It is clear that Charlie's clothes are important to him. He dresses well, and I know that it gives him a feeling of confidence to do so. That is his style. He is known for it, and he carries it off well.

Scott wears the same uniform every day. Loafers, well polished. Gray or beige slacks. A White or blue shirt. Interesting necktie. Scott thinks that this is appropriate, and he always looks professional. That is his style.

Greg works in an industry that seems to be devoid of neckties. Every day he wears slacks, and either a nice golf-type shirt, or a collared shirt, never unbuttoned too far. He never looks like he is headed for a picnic. That is his style.

I really don't have a specific opinion about how women should dress, having never been one. I am sure that the same rules apply, however, as listed above.

If your company has a dress code, you need to stick to it; it's not worth being rebellious about. You can stick to the rules and keep to your own style.

A sales VP that I know insists that all salesman wear ties whenever they will be visible to customers. He believes that knotting up that necktie is like putting on the armor, and preparing for battle. It's like putting on the uniform and getting ready for the big game. I like that analogy; it makes sense to me. Certainly, companies have the right to state their own dress code, and so I was surprised when I met with a gentleman of his employ, who was sans a tie for his workday. I asked him about this, and he spouted a long line of rhetoric about the fact that he is not a child who needs to be told what to wear, and that his customers didn't seem to mind.
"But isn't it a rule?" I asked. He was certainly aware of the rule, and disobeyed it whenever possible. Then he asked me, "Do you really think that what I wear makes a difference to customers?" I answered that I honestly thought it might. "How so?" he inquired, wanting more to defend himself than learn anything. Since he asked, I felt obligated to answer.
"Because you look like crap," I said.

"Your shirt is wrinkled, and your pants are too tight. Your shoes are dirty."
"So?" he asked defiantly.
I told him that people only know what we present to them, and that I was sure that he could, with very little effort, do far better. I also told him to stop focusing on the rule, instead of the reasoning behind it.
What the VP wanted was a sales force that looked professional, and displayed confidence and success.
I cannot see any way to argue with that.

Gifts and Entertainment.

I want to get this out of the way early. I don't believe in buying gifts for customers or entertaining them. I see it as unnecessary, and sometimes harmful.

Let me explain my position.

I have had sales jobs where it was expected that you spend money on customers by taking them to lunch, or dinner, or golf, or the casino, a ball game. My employer expected it, and it became an expectation of the customers. It was an expense, and there was money in the sales budget for it.
I have also worked for a company that felt as though if you wanted to take a customer to lunch, or dinner, then go ahead. It's your time, and your money. There was no budget, and no reimbursement for this. Any entertaining of customers during work hours, like taking customers golfing, was not okay. Golf was not considered work. There were no company tickets for sporting events.

When I first joined this company, with their seemingly unusual culture, I disagreed with it, but I also noticed that it couldn't really have been a belief that I held tightly, because I wasn't willing to spend *my own* money on customers.

Of course, it came up sometime with customers. Some actually seemed to think that they deserved these perks; it was owed to them. I was surprised at how shamelessly some customers held out their hands.

It forced me to recall times when I was a customer and I had been on the receiving end of a fat sales budget. I had to accept that I liked it; I particularly enjoyed the great seats I occasionally got for baseball games, but that it really didn't make any difference in my buying habits.

My position changed more as I found myself defending this culture. I would explain that my employer saw it this way: The money spent on entertainment could be better used in developing new products, and that was really more important in the long run. I thought it was interesting that customers never expected me to use *my own* money for this, and I could also recall how many had the "sky is the limit" attitude, when I would take them to dinner at my employer's expense, at previous jobs.

I believe that I never really sold one more thing because I spent money on customers, and that I never lost business because I didn't.

I also had to admit that my entertaining also sometimes put me with people I didn't necessarily enjoy, and took me away from my family.

Not having the "crutch" of the fat expense account forced me to find other ways to get to know customers, which I learned to do. It also made me realize that when I would occasionally take a customer to lunch, it was because I had some success, and it was clear that I was saying "Thank you."

This is a matter of style. I am not attempting to persuade you toward my own beliefs, but I am encouraging you to think about it, and think about it specifically, in this way.

If you are going to entertain customers, act as though you are using your own money. You'll be forced to decide if it's worth it.

Name-dropping and a Storytelling.

This is another matter of style. For some, talking about what the guy down the road did, or talking about the success that someone else in the same community had, seems a little too unprofessional and colloquial.

There is a particular reason that I bring up this topic, however. As you have read, I maintain that it is crucial to selling that you develop excellent questioning skills, so that you can ultimately focus on a particular problem that the customer wants to solve, and you have the solution. This is clearly a key element in any need satisfaction selling discipline.

As a sales trainer on this very topic, I have seen some salesmen struggle mightily with having the patience and the skill to ask all of those questions that bring a customer to a point where he says, "Yes, that's a problem for me, and I want to do something about it."

I developed what I think is the *second best* way, to get to the same place. If you just can't master the best way, perhaps an alternative will suit you. That was my reasoning when I went to work on this point that seems so difficult for some. As I was first thinking on the topic, I discovered that most of the trainees that struggled with probing questions, were pre-loaded toward talking, as soon as they felt like they knew what ball park they were in.

I call this technique a Statement of Opportunity. You use this when you perceive, by hearing or seeing, a problem that you can help with. In fact, you know that you have solved this problem for others, in what seems like a similar situation.

Several salesmen have told me that this technique helps them when they observe a customer going about his business in ways that seem primitive or uninformed. In the past, they said something not too different from, "Hey knucklehead, you're doing it wrong!" They recognize that this is a difficult mistake to recover from.

Darren was a youthful looking salesman, even younger in appearance than his 22 years. He was a bright guy and eager to learn.

Shortly after his initial product training, he listened to a senior manager talk about just how foolish it is, in this day and age, for customers to go about their work using ancient technology. He was obviously a persuasive speaker, because Darren became a devoted disciple and believer.

In sales training, Darren, (who was too young to know when to keep his mouth shut, and make himself a sales legend) told the class all about what he had learned from his product training. He continued with the facts that he had learned from the persuasive manager. His story continued, by telling us all that he visited a factory just a week after this enlightenment, and after quick observation, he began telling a seasoned plant manager, more than twenty years his senior, effectively this:

"Hey! You know you're doing this wrong."

Darren continued by telling us that he began his lecture, one that he had down word for word, as learned from the dynamic manager.

I asked Darren this question. "So, how did he like you calling him a bonehead?"

"That's just the thing," Darren replied. " I was trying to do what I was told, and the guy got so mad that he led me out to the lobby by my ear."

Following the laughter from the other sales people, someone suggested to Darren that some stories are better left untold.

I promised Darren that I would never stop telling this story.

Darren had his beliefs and his passion and enthusiasm in the right place, but the net effect was somewhat undesirable. Maybe a Statement of Opportunity would have been more helpful. Remember that it is *only* an opportunity. You are acting on a hunch.

After your well-prepared presentation, you need to carefully uncover whether the customer sees himself in a similar situation, and therefore he might benefit from knowing more about the proposed solution.

Perhaps if Darren had said something like:

I can see what you're doing over there in the widget department. We have worked with lots of customers in similar situations. I would like to tell you about ABC Industries, and what our product did for them. Basically, we were able to reduce manufacturing time by 15%, and in a way that the floor workers found easy to embrace, because it was better for them. Want to know more about it?

This gets to the point quickly, and encourages customers only to learn more about a potential advantage that they might get. By including the name, you are pointing to something that the customer can see, that may well apply to him also.

I was helping to introduce a brand-new product. Some of its features were brilliant and revolutionary.
I knew of a customer that I thought this product would be perfect for. I also knew that my contact was in love with his current supplier and solution, but I also knew that this new product would be far better for him. I was that sure.
*I had known the customer for long enough to know that he was bright, opinionated and successful. I believed that if I introduced a new product to him, he would be looking for what was wrong with it, and I hoped to avoid that conversation. I called for an appointment to discuss a new **idea**.*

"We have been working on a new widgetizer for some time," I began.
"We started by ignoring every other current solution, and focused on what we believed were the biggest challenges for widget makers.

We think that for the person that uses a widgetizer, it has to be so simple to use, that he can learn it by using it.
We think this is important, because of our belief that they would be reluctant about learning about something completely different, when their current widgetizers seemed just fine."

He agreed with the idea.

"We also thought that it had to have a lot of similar characteristics to existing widgetizers. By this I mean that it has to look similar, and even include a mode of operation that gave them the ability to do things in 'the old way', to help them to comfortably make the transition to something far more powerful."

He agreed with the idea.

"Also for the user, we wanted some way in which he could feel comfortable in using a highly advanced and automated product. By this, I mean we wanted them to always feel that they had control. Our belief is that if they think that the product can get away from them, they won't embrace it."

He agreed with the idea.

"For owners and management, our goal was to provide a widgetizer that you could immediately see would be, at minimum, twice as fast as current widgetizers."

He thought that was a great idea.

"We had to invent some things to meet all of the criteria, and we have."

He asked if he could see a product demonstration, but I reminded him that this was very new, and none had been delivered as yet. I also let him know that there were only certain people that we would be talking to initially, and that these were people that understood the risks and rewards of being early adopters of new technology.
I had some photographs, but product literature did not exist. I had been provided with a product simulator that would show him all of the fundamentals. He was anxious to see this. As I went through the demonstration to show him, step by step, how it achieved each of the conditions that we believed, and he agreed, were vital.

And, he ordered one, even though this was an untested, brand-new product that included some amazing technology that I could only do my best to explain.

This is another example of a Statement of Opportunity. You set out your ideas and beliefs, to see if they are shared, and would be useful to the prospect. You talk about the problems that the product is intended to alleviate, to see if this is an obstacle for him, in his world.

A Statement of Opportunity, like any presentation, needs to be refined and powerful. But it also is a way of telling a story. If you like to illustrate and teach customers by the use of stories, rather than questioning to a need, it might be for you.

If you feel comfortable saying to a customer, "We recently worked with ABC, who does similar things to you. I would like to tell you about our success there. They were fairly reluctant at first, but it has worked out pretty well. Maybe it's a good idea for you to."
If you do, Statements of Opportunity might be a technique for you to consider.

If you find that being able to say things like, "XYZ just bought a new copier from us, because they needed a faster machine, and the ability to collate, would that be helpful to you?" as a way of getting into the meat of the product, then you might consider developing your own Statements of Opportunity.

Just keep in mind that all it provides is the chance to demonstrate a solution to a hunch that you have about some problems that they have, and would like to do something about. You need to hear them say that they have this problem and are looking for a solution in order to go forward. Without that, it's just a story.

In any case, this is just a suggestion. It's another way of getting product ideas in front of a customer, and avoiding confrontation. It's another style, and I never argue about matters of style.

Manners

Well-mannered people are not wimps, as some would have you believe.

Most professional people, it seems to me, are well mannered. Inversely, there are not a lot of truly successful people that are arrogant buttheads. It is awfully difficult for people to want to promote you, bring business your way, or do business with you at all, if you have given them cause to dislike you.

I want to be very careful in what I am saying here. I was once chastised severely for not being aggressive enough. To me, it seems that being too aggressive, is much like being pushy, which I dislike in people, and probably you do also.

I am highly in favor of being assertive, and proactive. These are things that you can be, and still be mannerly and thoughtful.

I am most aware of the need for good manners, when I think about how salesmen often have to go about our business.

Often, we are intruders. We show up, or call, on our own schedule. It is unlikely that your contact could get away with telling his boss that he was going to just sit around idly today, in case a salesman came by.

When we interject ourselves into the lives of our prospects, they were, most likely, doing something called "their job."

They had to stop doing "their job," to meet with you, or talk to you. After you leave, they will go back to doing their job.

Don't get all flustered if a guy just won't take the time to see you, just because you happened into his world. Isn't it possible that he is in the middle of a crisis, or a meeting? Might he be under a lot of pressure to meet a deadline?

If you look at things from his perspective, it should be easy to react in a courteous enough way to accept being shut out today, but leaving the door open for next time.

I sometimes forget to ask the most basic question, on an unannounced visit or phone call, which is, "Is this a good time for you?"

I am encouraging you to be courteously professional enough to accept that right now might not be perfect for your prospect.

This should apply also, when you show up for an appointment, and the customer is not available. Isn't it possible that something changed drastically from the time that the appointment was set, until the time for the appointment came?

Be courteous about having to accept the inevitable sometimes. If you don't, you will most likely be viewed as a thoughtless jerk. (This is bad.)

Please don't see this in conflict to any earlier comments that I have made. You still need to drive the process; you still need to close every call.
It is still true that a process begins when you make a decision to do business with someone.
You can be proactive and assertive, and still be polite. If a person is not available for you *right now*, keep after things until there is a good time for you both.
And don't burn the bridge behind you by being a jerk because someone wouldn't stop everything to see you.

A Final Word

If it is your "style," to lie to customers, please quit sales now. Eventually you will have to stop selling anyway, either because your company doesn't employ liars, or because your sales levels won't support your lifestyle, now that you have learned that you can manipulate someone once for a sale, but not twice.

This lying also includes, in varying degrees, half-truths, letting customers believe that your products do something that they don't because they misunderstand, bold and hollow statements of rhetoric, ignoring customers once they catch on to you, and blaming the organization for not delivering on something that you made up. The truth resonates loud enough to build a career on.

I was at a trade show, and had just completed a sale that was pretty juicy. When we were through with the paperwork, and I was thanking the customer, who happened to be the owner of the company, the president of my own company walked by. I introduced them, and let the big boss know about the sale that had just been completed.
The customer said to the president, "Let me ask you something. How good is the service on these things?"
I felt the sale slipping away when he responded, "It's pretty good."
"Pretty good?" my soon-to- be- ex- customer responded.
"Well, It's pretty hard to provide great field service. There is just this uneven demand for service, and it's hard to staff for it. We don't want customers to wait too long, but we can't afford to have idle servicemen either. Sometimes we're really prompt, and sometimes people can be down for a day or two. That can be too long, because people start to depend on our equipment. As the president of the company, I get those phone calls sometimes, and I know it puts people in a predicament."

There was a long silence. The customer looked at me, pointed toward the president, and said, "An honest man."

The customer remarked on that story to me several times, in the next few months. I'll bet he never forgot it, and apparently, I haven't either, although it occurred 25 years ago.

In sales, the truth has to be good enough. People can handle it, and they can sniff it out when sales people say things like, "Our service is great. We're the best in the business."

So, if you want to stretch the truth, lie, and manipulate to get business, I can assure you, by all that I have seen, that it will be a short career.
In addition, you are making it harder for the good guys. They have to deal with the reputation that you give to sales people, even after your career has become one where you get to ask customers:

"You want fries with that?"

Chapter 13

Some comments to, and about, Sales Managers.

If you are a salesman, then I would like to remind you that there are only two kinds of bosses: great ones, or idiots. At least that's what salesmen always seem to say. The only words of advice that I can offer are these:

1. If you have a great boss, get the most from him while you can. Chances are that others will notice his greatness also, and he will move along to another company, or up in the organization. If it occurs to you, thank him, if he or she has earned it.
2. Sometimes you will be stuck with a boss that truly is a hindrance, or an irritation to you. Stop whining, and deal with it. It happens to all sales people sometime in their career.

The real intent of this chapter is to make a few observations or suggestion for sales managers.

Sales managers sometimes do more harm than good to salesmen. This is particularly true of the manager that is always focused on the sales that have been lost, or are still in process. In either case, no sale has occurred, and the weak manager grinds away on the salesman about what he *should* do, or what he *should have done,* or worse yet, *what he would have done, when he was the top salesman in the whole wide world.*
The reason I say this is that so often the interaction that managers have with salesmen is away from the sale, and therefore they come to conclusions based on what the salesman tells them, and what they believe from experience.

It is my view that many sales are lost, and many sales careers ruined, by managers that either micro-manage the salesmen, or constantly provide negative feedback. Sales people need to find ways to feel confident, and this does not come from customers very often. Therefore, they need to develop self-confidence in order to keep on working through the process, day by day by day. If the manager closest to them is also a confidence eroder, there just is not much good happening in the life of the salesman.

I was once watching my son at a Little League baseball game. A ground ball was hit to the shortstop. It was a slightly tougher than routine chance, but it should have been handled. It wasn't.
Think about what was going through the mind of that twelve-year-old boy at that moment. Certainly he was aware that he had a booted a ball in front of his friends and family.
I was appalled when his manager began screaming at the boy from the dugout.
If someone is hollering things like, "Concentrate!" and "Keep your eye on the ball," they might be intended to be words of encouragement, but they have the opposite effect when they are screamed out, and for everyone to hear.

I could see the look of humiliation on the boy's face.
My son was the next batter.
I said to the person next to me that if he hit the ball to the shortstop he'd be on base for sure. "Why do you say that?' he asked.
" The shortstop is the best player on that team."
"Right now he isn't." I said. "Right now he's been humiliated and the only thing on his mind is that everybody knows what a poor fielder he is. The coach did that to him."
I watched my son hit the next pitch right between his legs.

Many times, we achieve what we achieve, not because of our ability, but because of our desire, and our self-confidence.

If you are a fabulous sales manager, I salute you, and you needn't read on. For the rest, I am going to mention some negatives to avoid.

1. Sales managers are generally middle managers. Therefore, they are not in a position to create policy, and policy is the responsibility of top management. Sometimes, managers have to explain policies, and why they are important to the company, but it is never the job of the manager to interpret policy. Managers that tell a salesman what policies to avoid, or say things like "Just worry about what I want," are teaching the salesman to be bad employees, and telling them

that senior management doesn't know what it's doing. If you want to argue about the rules, argue with your boss. Let him know what's wrong with the policy. One of you is liable to learn something.

2. **Don't give sales people work to do for your benefit**. By this I mean, don't have the salesmen working on reports or data, just so you can know what they are doing. If you need to know what is up with a salesman, you should be able to learn everything from the notes and data that you are encouraging him to keep for himself. If you can't do this, then he doesn't know what's going on in his territory any way. Be a good boss; create and support an efficient system of record keeping.

3. **Leave them alone**. If you are a good and helpful manager, you will know this because your direct reports will seek you out for advice. They will ask you to spend time in the field with them. These are important things for you to be doing, if, and only if, the sales person wants help from you. If he doesn't, and he is failing, that's on him, not you. His job is to meet the goals that you have set for him, using the tools and resources available to him. Your job is to fill the territory with someone competent to meet. and exceed those goals.

I have heard plenty of complaints from salesmen that their manager calls them up and says things like, "You got any orders for me?"

Who exactly are the orders for? Are they for the manager? How exactly does that phone call help a salesman or a customer?

If you are calling a salesman more than twice a month, just to bug him for orders, you are wasting your time, and the salesman's time.

Don't most salesmen know how to let everyone in the world know when they have some success?

4. **Be fair, not equal.**

   There are certain rules that apply to everyone. These are called company policies, and they should always be applied evenly. However, there are other things that should be applied based on success. The best salesmen are already working harder than the others. They are working longer and working smarter. So, look for random occasions when they can be rewarded thusly.

Perhaps you buy them a bottle of their favorite wine, or treat the salesman and their spouse to dinner. Maybe they need a little personal time, and you look the other way. Perhaps there is a trade show that needs setting up, and you give the job to the less successful performers. Why should you do this? Because they have earned a little slack, and some benefit, not for their efforts, but for their results. One more thing, make sure that everyone knows about it; so that you can be clear that it is not favoritism, but a reward that has been earned.

5. **Be a coach, not an all-star**.
   Salesmen need training in order to be competent in each important area of their job. Most companies have a training program for the newbies that, as a manager, you should support. Even the best salesmen need support, objective criticism, and fresh ideas. That is what you, as a coach, should provide. What you should not do is to spend coaching opportunities regaling them with stories about your considerable prowess back when you were on the street. You might relate some things you learned by way of story, but do everything you can to use the time with them coaching. Keep it about them, not you.

6. **Do the things that they can't, or shouldn't.**
   Position yourself with the salespeople that you support, to take on the dirty work. Get directly involved with nasty service problems or tough collection issues when the salesman needs your help. Take their complaints to upper management when necessary, and report back to them. Salesmen often have a great sense of when the boss should be involved. Accept those jobs when they give them to you. Work on a relationship that insures that they will come to you when they need this kind of help. Try to become the kind of manager that the salesman wants to bring in for help with a tough situation, and the kind that he will feel proud to bring to the big meetings.
   You manage things, and lead people.

7. **Promote group input, not just yours.**
   This seems to be a problem for those managers that also do silly things like try to control everything, encourage salesmen

to keep secrets from corporate types, and generally try to create their own little fiefdom to rule over.

Salesmen need a boss, and they require training and guidance, to be sure. Just don't hinder the salesmen from going to each other for help. It will sometimes be better help than you can give, since it comes from a guy facing the same challenges. Also, another salesman should really know more about what's happening with customers, because he is closer to them, and therefore closer to the buzz. So, let them go to each other for advice and fresh ideas, and information about customers and competitors. There is a huge benefit that salesmen, particularly younger salesmen, get from this. The very best salesmen also seem to be willing to help the most. That is good for everyone.

Salesmen spend a great deal of time working alone. Promote the camaraderie that comes from helping your fellow workers. It's good for business.

A final thought. Please don't ever use the words, "My guys," or "My salespeople." They don't belong to you, and it is insulting to the people that report to you.

We generally work better with people, than for people.

The Author would like to thank lots of people.

First, I would like to thank you, if you bought this book. If you are reading someone else's copy, I sort of thank you, and wish you well in your sales career anyway.

Thanks to my wife, who helps provide the time, by not insisting that I get a real job.

Thanks to Rich, for teaching me to think, whether I wanted to or not.

To Steve, for being a steady and inspiring leader, and for having far more vision than your average marketing dweeb.

To John, a sales manager who does everything better than everyone else, and is therefore a great example.

To Paul, who knew how to get everyone going in the same direction.

To Paul, who knew how to get everyone running around the barn, even if they didn't know why.

To Frank and Peter, who told me I should write this book, and to my Dad, who told me I could.

You guys know who you are.

I am also very grateful to Jim Seward and Denny Johnson. Both of them made me believe that good guys can be great salesmen. They inspired me, in the way that they do business, to give sales a try for myself.

About the author.

Dennis Coleman resides in rural Chester County, Pennsylvania.

His writing includes a great deal of ranting on the subjects of his own choice and whim, along with various works of fiction. His fictional writing reflects his love for the American convention of the short story.

When he is not writing books and stories, he also enjoys writing and performing music.

This particular book reflects the author's wish to provide a little help to those who work in the field of sales.

Dennis is a student of the many and varied methods of selling that are based on what some call need satisfaction. In addition, he believes that sales should be embraced as a helping profession, therefore requiring sales people to understand the particular circumstances of each customer.
He also thinks that sales can be fun.

www.denniscoleman.net

www.ingramcontent.com/pod-product-compliance
Lightning Source LLC
Chambersburg PA
CBHW051833040426
42447CB00006B/504